Dinosaurs to Dung Beetles: Expeditions Through Time

Guide to the Sternberg Museum of Natural History

by Gregory A. Liggett

Sternberg Museum of Natural History, Publisher
Dr. Jerry R. Choate, Director

Fort Hays State University
Dr. Edward H. Hammond, President

Published by the Sternberg Museum of Natural History, a department of Fort Hays State University
3000 Sternberg Drive
Hays, Kansas 67601-2006
www.fhsu.edu/sternberg

FORT HAYS STATE
UNIVERSITY

Printed in the United States of America

Cover photograph of the Sternberg Museum
Tyrannosaurus rex by Charlie Riedel

Library of Congress Card Number: 00-112084
ISBN 0-9707714-0-1

First Edition

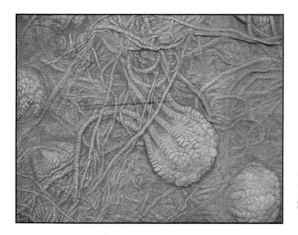

Border across the bottom is from the *Uintacrinus* slab displayed at the Sternberg Museum (fig. 80).

Fort Hays State University
Mission Statement

Fort Hays State University, a regional university principally serving western Kansas, is dedicated to providing instruction within a computerized environment in the arts and sciences, business, education, the health and life sciences, and agriculture. The university's primary emphasis is undergraduate liberal education, which includes the humanities, the fine arts, the social/behavioral sciences, and the natural/physical sciences. These disciplines serve as the foundation of all programs. Graduates are provided a foundation for entry into graduate school, for employment requiring well-developed analytical and communication skills, and for coping with global complexities of the 21st century.

Natural outgrowths of the university's primary emphasis include pre-professional, professional, master's, and education specialist programs. A statewide strategic focus of the university is the integration of computer and telecommunications technology with the educational environment and the work place.

Scholarship at FHSU is supported because it stimulates faculty and students, provides new knowledge, connects the disciplines, and builds bridges between teaching and learning while linking theory with practice to address the needs of society.

The university is responsible for providing public service to the community, the region, and the state of Kansas. Programs consistent with the university's academic and research activities emphasize the importance of FHSU as the cultural center of western Kansas.

For more information contact:

Fort Hays State University
600 Park Street
Hays, KS 67601-4099
(800) 628-FHSU
www.fhsu.edu

The Sternberg Museum would like to give you a complimentary newsletter subscription for 4 issues. Just clip or photocopy and mail the completed form to the address below.

Name _____

Address _____

City _____ State_____ ZIP _____

Phone _____ Email _____

Mail to: Sternberg Museum of Natural History
Newsletter Subscription
3000 Sternberg Drive
Hays, Kansas 67601

Acknowledgments & Dedication

I would like to thank many people who helped make this book a reality one way or another. Jerry Choate, Director of the Sternberg Museum of Natural History, has always been very supportive of this project and of me in general. I thank the staff of the Sternberg, who are, without exception, a dedicated bunch. I always knew that working at a museum is a labor of love and the Sternberg staff proves it every day. I thank each of them for their dedication.

My former advisors, Richard Zakrzewski, Chief Curator at the Sternberg, and Michael Nelson, Dean at University of Wisconsin-LaCrosse, both taught me a great deal about the science of paleontology and what it means to be a professional. Greg McDonald, of the National Park Service, encouraged me to pursue my interests, and did not try too hard to convince me there were no jobs in paleontology. Edward Hammond, President of Fort Hays State University, deserves special thanks, for without his drive to build the new home for the Sternberg Museum, this book would lack a starting place.

Several people helped with figures on short notice. Mitch Weber, Center for Teaching Excellence and Learning Technology at FHSU, helped with several pictures of the museum on campus as well as shooting some special photographs. Judy Salm, FHSU Archivist, allowed me access to the extensive collection of Sternberg photographs in her care. Hannan LaGarry, Conservation and Survey Division, University of Nebraska, Lincoln, worked hard on short notice to provide line drawings. The archivists at the Yale Peabody Museum and the American Museum of Natural History also provided images on short notice, and in some cases with little direction from the author.

David Meyer from the University of Cincinnati answered questions on *Uintacrinus*. Several people looked the text over and provided valuable comments; you know who you are.

This book is much improved by the inclusion of the wonderful paintings by Dan Varner. He generously allowed me to reproduce them, and they add a lot.

I would like to thank my best critic and the best editor I know, my wife, Cameron, who encourages me daily to do my best work. My daughter, Rebecca, also helped with some of the graphic work. I am deeply in debt to them both for their personal sacrifices during this book's production.

I owe much to my family who taught me a love of nature and the outdoors during many exciting childhood excursions. I dedicate this book to my brother, Scott. As children, I tormented him far too much. Now that he is bigger than I am, I want him to know that I have always been proud of him.

Contents

Sternberg Museum of Natural History
Floor Plans

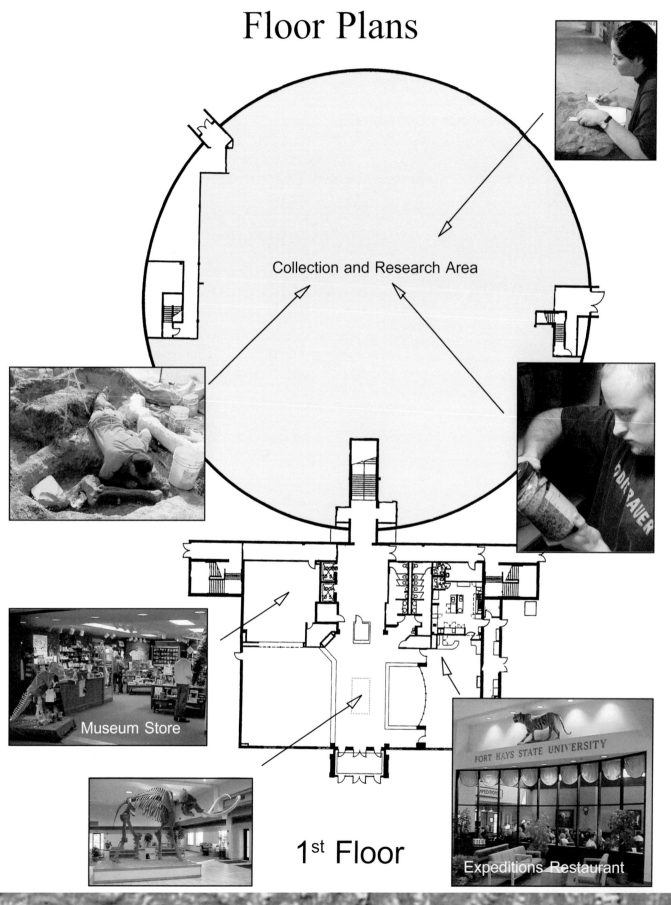

Collection and Research Area

Museum Store

1st Floor

Expeditions Restaurant

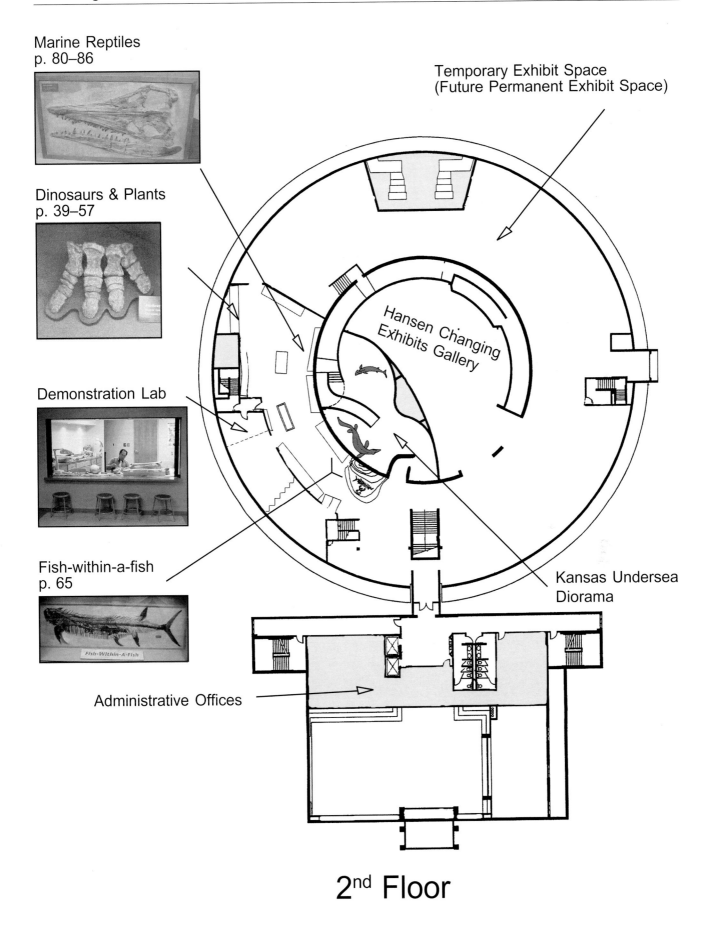

Marine Reptiles
p. 80–86

Dinosaurs & Plants
p. 39–57

Demonstration Lab

Fish-within-a-fish
p. 65

Administrative Offices

Temporary Exhibit Space
(Future Permanent Exhibit Space)

Hansen Changing
Exhibits Gallery

Kansas Undersea
Diorama

2nd Floor

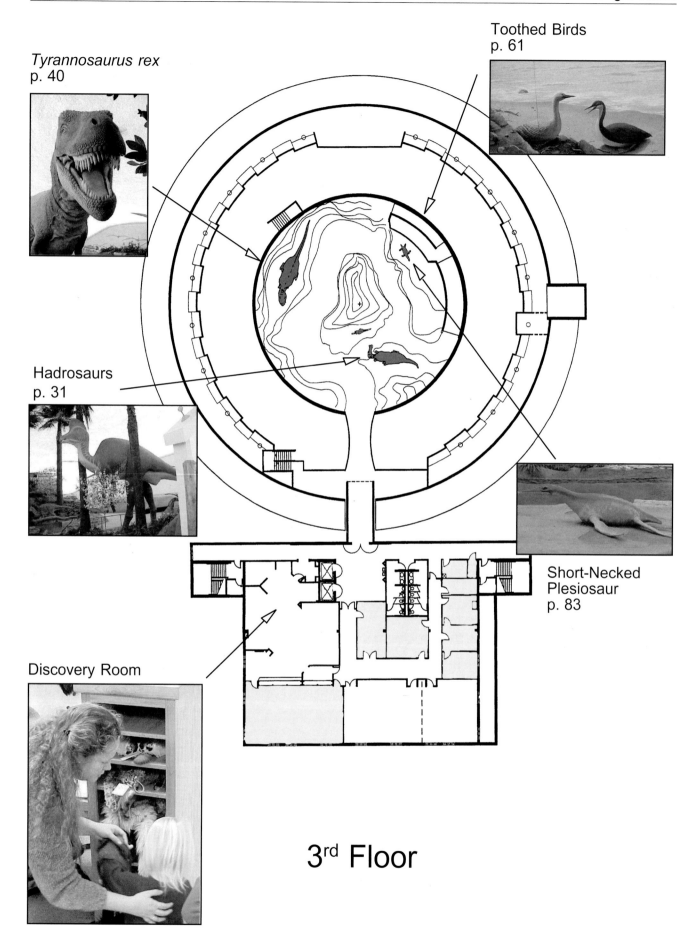

Tyrannosaurus rex
p. 40

Toothed Birds
p. 61

Hadrosaurs
p. 31

Short-Necked
Plesiosaur
p. 83

Discovery Room

3rd Floor

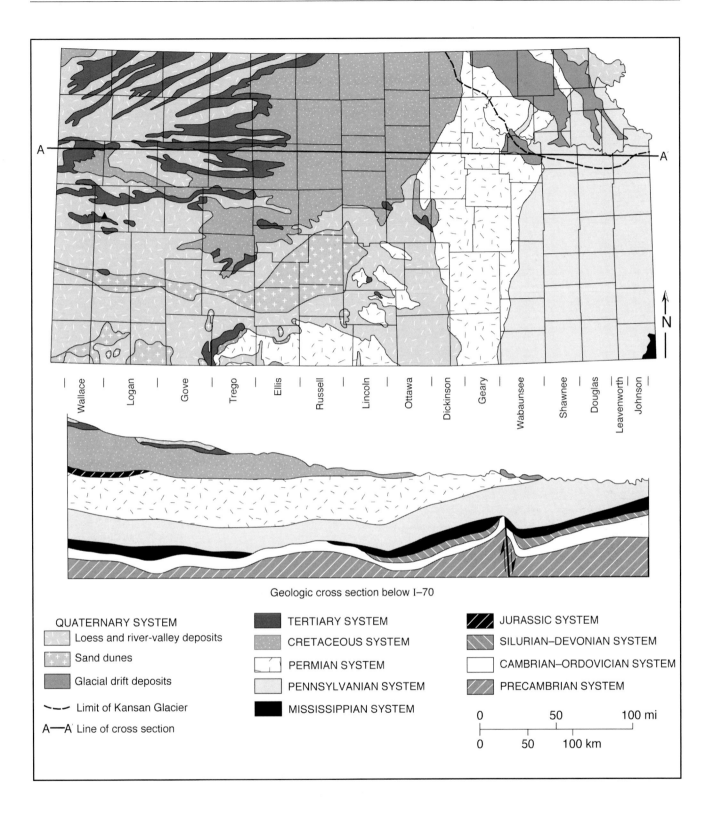

Geologic cross section below I–70

QUATERNARY SYSTEM

Loess and river-valley deposits

Sand dunes

Glacial drift deposits

Limit of Kansan Glacier

A——A' Line of cross section

TERTIARY SYSTEM

CRETACEOUS SYSTEM

PERMIAN SYSTEM

PENNSYLVANIAN SYSTEM

MISSISSIPPIAN SYSTEM

JURASSIC SYSTEM

SILURIAN–DEVONIAN SYSTEM

CAMBRIAN–ORDOVICIAN SYSTEM

PRECAMBRIAN SYSTEM

0   50   100 mi

0   50   100 km

Generalized Surface Geology
of Kansas

Preface

This book has been trying to write itself for several years. When I first came to Hays and began to explore the museum, I felt a deep sense of history, of being directly connected to events and noteworthy people in history. The idea to put that down in a book sprung to life in the back of my mind. The connections extend through my major professor, Richard Zakrzewski, who succeeded Myrl Walker, who succeeded George Sternberg, whose father Charles was one of the most prolific fossil hunters of all time, who worked with Edward D. Cope, who quarreled with O. C. Marsh in one of the most famous and bitterly personal public confrontations between scientists, and who was instrumental in the discovery of important fossils that tipped the balance of the scientific community to embrace the reality of biological evolution, which was published by Darwin…

Feeling this connection with all that has gone before provides me with a deep respect for the Sternberg Museum. I was fortunate to be in the right place at the right time. While I was finishing up my undergraduate and graduate degrees in Hays, the museum and university administration was seeking a new home for the museum. A building across town from the campus was identified and acquired to house the museum. I was involved with the development of that project from beginning to end. Today, the museum staff, the university, and the entire community of Hays can be proud of our collective accomplishment. The new museum is a tremendous step forward, yet another chapter in the history of science and the university.

This book, with over 100 figures and pictures, provides up-to-date answers on some aspects of paleobiology. How did *Tyrannosaurus rex* hunt, and how do we know? What is unique about the head of a *T. rex* that made it the most fearsome land predator ever? Did some dinosaurs live in herds? How might they have communicated? What did mosasaurs eat, and how did they live? What special adaptations did mosasaurs and plesiosaurs have for life in the sea? These and other questions pertinent to the Sternberg Museum of Natural History's exhibits and research are addressed here.

The title of this book is meant to encompass the broad stretch of topics connected to the museum. Dinosaurs are central to the early days of fossil collecting, and the Sternberg family collected their share. The stories of Late Cretaceous dinosaurs and other prehistoric animals are incorporated into the museum's permanent exhibits. Museum staff carefully chose which animals and stories to portray. Although a visit to the museum is not essential, this book is the story behind the exhibits, providing deeper meaning to almost every aspect displayed, modeled, and painted. Hopefully, the reader will gain a greater appreciation of the museum, and perhaps even a warm, satisfied feeling of understanding more than the average visitor.

The other side of the title, dung beetles, reflects another extreme in the museum's holdings and research. As a complete natural science museum we collect the large and small of nature, including plants, insects (like dung beetles), fishes, amphibians, reptiles, birds, and mammals of the Great Plains. Follow the story through 330 million years of geologic history, to the wild West, to dinosaur collecting in Canada, fossil collecting in Kansas, and the development of a museum at Fort Hays State University in Hays, Kansas.

Worldwide, natural science museums are increasingly important as conservation and environmental concerns come to the forefront of public policy. The Sternberg Museum is not an isolated attraction on the plains of western Kansas, but an important link and a participant in an international network of scientists exploring the natural world of the past, present, and future. Our scientists communicate their findings through professional papers and meetings, and likewise learn the latest information in their fields. The museum is on the verge of becoming one of the nation's preeminent public education and research facilities in the 21st century. Nothing could honor the museum's heritage more, and we are ready.

—Greg Liggett, Hays, Kansas January, 2001

Chapter 1
Beginnings

Where does a story begin? Behind every story lies another story, a series of events that lays the groundwork before a particular story can begin.

Do we start with the establishment of a small "museum room" in the first building on the campus of the new teachers' school in 1907 at Hays, Kansas? Do we begin with the recruitment of fossil collector George F. Sternberg to the staff of the college, because he so greatly enhanced the museum's collections? Perhaps we should look further back in time, at the early settlement of Kansas. An exciting history of scientific discovery and exploration connect the museum of today with the early pioneering days. Perhaps we need to look even further back in time, into "deep time" as geologists call it, to a moment when magnificent animals swam, flew, and crept—not over the vast prairie of today—but over and through the vast sea of yesterday.

March 13, 1999: The Grand Opening

On March 13, 1999, the Sternberg Museum re-opened its doors and entered a new era in its history. In 1991, Fort Hays State University president Dr. Edward H. Hammond had seen potential in an oddly shaped building that Hays residents usually just called "the dome." Museum and university staff worked many long hours over eight years planning, designing, and implementing every aspect of the building's transformation, from where the walls should go in the collection rooms to what the public experiences in the galleries. Generous donors caught the vision and contributed the financial means to complete the project. The city of Hays, Ellis County, and the Kansas legislature recognized the potential of the new museum to Hays and the state of Kansas. The university perceived the significance of the new museum facility to scientists around the world.

To Prehistory: Where the Story Begins

The Sternberg Museum's history encompasses events that span at least the last 330 million years. We'll visit a variety of subjects as we flesh out the museum's story. We'll spotlight some of the many hidden connections. Some of these connections are in the exhibit galleries and the Discovery Room, places where the public routinely goes. Some of the connections are in the "ranges" that house the research collections, places visitors seldom see. And some of the connections are intangible events in our collective prehistoric and historic past. The story is so large that there is something here for everyone. It is a fantastic story!

Figure 1. *George F. Sternberg works on the Fish-within-a-fish in the museum's recreation of the dig.*

Figure 2. As with man-made statues, natural monuments are also subject to the erosional ravages of time. George Sternberg took this photograph of Cobra Rock, near Castle Rock, in Gove County, about 1940. The monument fell in 1998.

Figure 3. *Completed in 1912, this was the first standing mount the Sternbergs ever attempted. It is a brontothere that was found in Wyoming. It was mounted for the National Museum of Natural Sciences in Ottawa, Canada.*

Chapter 2
Long Ago & Far Away

Before the Sternberg Museum opened in its new facility, before George F. Sternberg settled in Hays, before the museum room was established in the library of the teachers' college, before Europeans fenced the west, before the first human inhabitants of the Great Plains arrived from the Siberian steppes…we need to go back in time 330 million years…

Plate Tectonics

Geologists divide Earth's history into named segments (fig. 4). In a calendar year we understand where October falls in relation to the other months. Likewise, geologists communicate about the deep past with terms like "Mesozoic" and "Cretaceous." The public most often hears terms from the time divisions known as periods (fig. 5). Unlike our calendar months, however, the geologic periods are not of equal duration.

Three hundred and thirty million years before the present places us in the Late Mississippian Period. The world looks strange to us. Not even the continents look familiar. In fact, Kansas is at the bottom of a tropical ocean in the Southern Hemisphere, not too far from the equator! The landmasses that will become North America and Europe are joined to form a continent called Laurasia. South America, Africa, Antarctica, and India combine to form another southern continent called Gondwana. And Laurasia and Gondwana are on a collision course of global proportions.

The crust of the earth is not a solid envelope, but rather it is like the surface of broken eggshell over a hardboiled egg. The crust and the uppermost layer of the underlying mantle collectively make up the lithosphere, which is broken into large units called plates. Below the lithospheric plates is the asthenosphere, a part of the mantle where the rocks can bend and flow because of the great pressure and heat of the Earth's interior. As the plates glide over the asthenosphere, they jostle

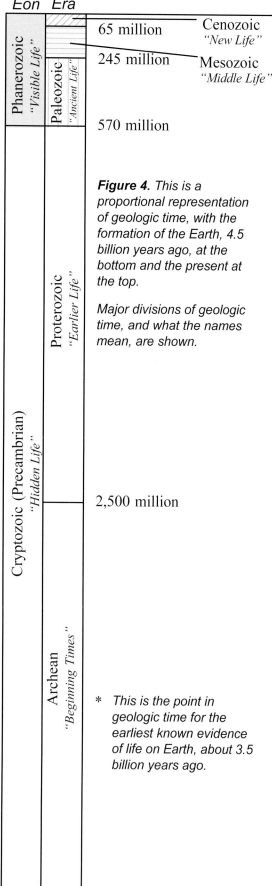

Eon   Era

		65 million	Cenozoic *"New Life"*
		245 million	Mesozoic *"Middle Life"*
		570 million	

Figure 4. *This is a proportional representation of geologic time, with the formation of the Earth, 4.5 billion years ago, at the bottom and the present at the top.*

Major divisions of geologic time, and what the names mean, are shown.

2,500 million

*   *This is the point in geologic time for the earliest known evidence of life on Earth, about 3.5 billion years ago.*

Phanerozoic *"Visible Life"*

Paleozoic *"Ancient Life"*

Proterozoic *"Earlier Life"*

Cryptozoic (Precambrian) *"Hidden Life"*

Archean *"Beginning Times"*

neighboring plates. One of three possible interactions between the plates takes place.

First, the plates may slip past one another. When this happens, the plates are pressed up against each other and friction resists the movements. Stresses build up until finally the resistance of the friction is overcome, and movement occurs, usually in short bursts. The result is felt as an earthquake. Energy is released as the ground moves under our feet. This can be experienced today along the coast of southern California at the famed San Andreas and other faults. Here the North American and Pacific plates slide past one another in a global friction contest. When the tension is released, Californians feel the effects, sometimes with devastating results.

Instead of sliding past each other, plates can move away from each other. The line between the separating plates, called a rift, is usually volcanically active as magma wells up from below. Iceland is a volcanic island that straddles the Mid-Atlantic Rift, and evidence of Iceland's volcanic origins can be seen in the numerous hot springs that the island is famous for. Up and down the Atlantic basin, like a seam on a baseball, the rift runs generally north and south as the continents of the Eastern and Western Hemispheres separate. This continual separation means that, in 1492, Christopher Columbus sailed a few feet fewer than do modern ships crossing the same ocean.

The third option in plate interaction is that the two plates can be driven together by the internal forces of the earth. As with any two masses that collide, something has to give. One plate may be driven over the top of the other with the subordinate plate being subducted beneath the superior plate. The subordinate plate is forced towards Earth's center, and when it descends deeply enough it melts under the great heat of the planet's interior. The molten rock makes its way back toward the surface, resulting in a chain of volcanic mountains paralleling the subduction zone. North America's Cascade Range, including Mt. St. Helens, is such a volcanic situation. There, North America rides over the Juan de Fuca Plate.

Pangea & Panthalassa

In the Late Mississippian Period, Laurasia and Gondwana rode their plates, crashed together, and became welded into one giant supercontinent called Pangea (from the Greek *pan* meaning "all" and the Greek *geios* meaning "of the earth;" so Pangea literally means "all the earth"). It was surrounded by the world-wide ocean called Panthalassa (Greek *thalassikos* meaning the sea). Pangea and Panthalassa (fig. 6) existed for almost 100 million years. During the Mississippian, Pennsylvanian, and Permian periods, Kansas was west-coast real estate. Located on the northwestern edge of Pangea, Kansas was awash beneath the Panthalassa waves. Sediment deposited at the bottom of the sea later became layers of limestone and shale. These very rocks can be seen at the surface of eastern Kansas today. In them are the remains of many diverse shelled invertebrates that lived in the Panthalassa Ocean.

Prior to these events, plants and animals had made their way onto land. The first animals to fully conquer the land were the insects and similar arthropods of Early Devonian Period (about 400 million years ago). The first vertebrate animals to move ashore were primitive amphibians in the Late Devonian (about 367 million years ago), and they gave rise to the first primitive reptiles soon after that.

Two groups of early reptiles were important later on in evolutionary history: the synapsids and the diapsids. These groups are distinguished by the number and

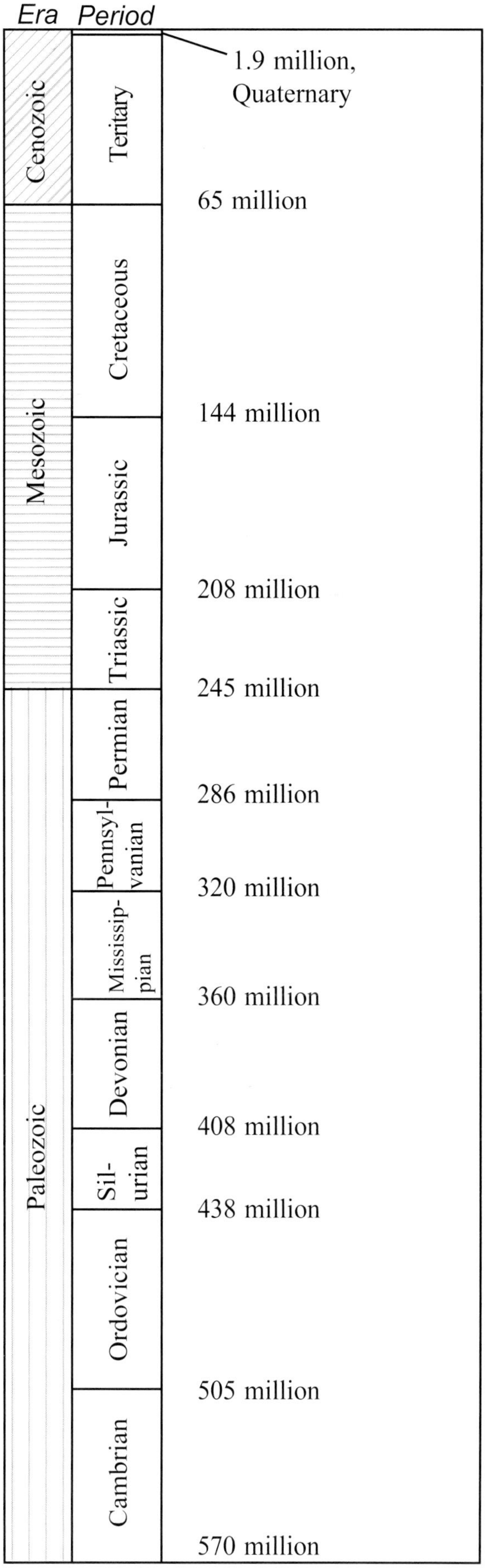

Figure 5. *The chart at the right is a proportional representation of just the Phanerozoic Eon, the last 570 million years. At the beginning of the Paleozoic Era, organisms evolved hard parts, like shells, that allowed their remains to become fossilized as visible evidence of their existance.*

During the Paleozoic Era, almost all the major groups of life forms diversified, including the first vertebrates.

The Mesozoic Era is sometimes called the "Age of Dinosaurs" because that is when they dominated the land.

Dinosaurs and many other groups of organisms became extinct at the end of the Cretaceous Period, 65 million years ago, and the "Age of Mammals" began with the Cenozoic Era.

Era	Period	
Cenozoic	Teritary	1.9 million, Quaternary
		65 million
Mesozoic	Cretaceous	
		144 million
	Jurassic	
		208 million
	Triassic	
		245 million
Paleozoic	Permian	
		286 million
	Pennsyl-vanian	
		320 million
	Mississip-pian	
		360 million
	Devonian	
		408 million
	Sil-urian	
		438 million
	Ordovician	
		505 million
	Cambrian	
		570 million

Figure 6. This series of figures depicts the geographic configuration of the continents from the Permian Period through the Late Cretaceous Period. The outlines reflect the approximate edge of the continental crust, not necessarily the coastline.

During the Late Permian Period (right), Pangea was the supercontinent formed by all the world's continental masses. Parts of Kansas were under shallow seas, where large areas of limestone were deposited that can be seen today in the Flint Hills. There was a large basin of marine water that dried over time and left behind evaporite minerals like salt and gypsum. These minerals are mined today in the south-central part of Kansas.

The Tethys Sea bordered eastern Africa, southern Asia, and northern India and Australia. The rest of the global ocean was called Panthalassa.

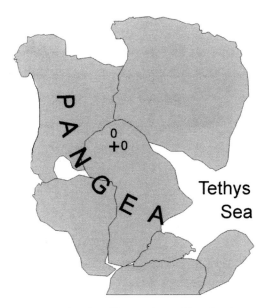

Late Permian Period

By the Late Triassic Period (left), the continents reversed course and began tearing Pangea apart. The southern continents that formed Gondwana broke apart into the modern continents of Africa, Antarctica, South America, and the Indian subcontinent.

India began its trek from the west coast of Africa to slam into Asia. The Gulf Coast of North America was opened, and the Atlantic basin was just starting to open between North America and Eurasia.

Late Triassic Period

By the Late Cretaceous Period (right), Africa and South America were seperated by the growing Atlantic Ocean, but North America and Eurasia were still connected in the as-yet-incomplete development of the Atlantic. India was continuing its northward migration and soon would crash into southern Asia, pushing up the Himalaya Moutains.

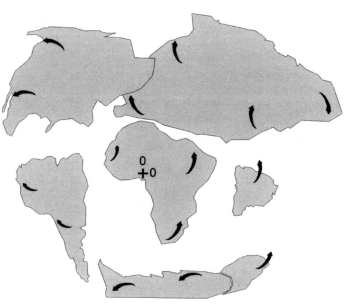

Late Cretaceous Period

arrangement of openings in the skull (fig. 7), but for our story what is important is that the two groups gave rise to separate lineages of later vertebrates. The synapsids formed a group called the mammal-like reptiles, and diverged into many primitive forms and ultimately into the modern mammals themselves. The diapsids gave rise to most of the modern reptiles, as well as the group that includes dinosaurs and birds. This divergence took place about 300 million years ago in the Pennsylvanian Period, and at first the synapsid branch dominated among the land-dwellers. However, for some reason, the synapsid animals fell upon hard times and almost became extinct. That circumstance opened the door for the diapsids to take control of the landscape beginning in the Triassic. They ruled the land for the next 150 million years.

While this biological drama was being played out on land, the supercontinent of Pangea reversed its course and began tearing apart in the mid-Triassic. Laurasia separated from Gondwana; then North and South America ripped away from Europe and Africa, opening up a new ocean: the Atlantic. Rocks that preserve evidence for these events, and the events of the next 160 million years, are not exposed at the surface in Kansas. But we know from the rock record at other places that the continents gradually moved toward their modern positions. And on those continents, a group that had descended from the diapsid reptiles came to dominate the land. They evolved into many wondrous forms, some with unbelievable size. That group is now known as the dinosaurs.

The Late Cretaceous & the Shallow Sea

The next rock record at the surface in Kansas is from the latest of the Early and the Late Cretaceous Period, about 100 to 65 million years ago. These rocks tell a story of a second time when Kansas was beachfront property (fig. 8). This time, however, there were differences. Kansas was not on the west coast of the continent; rather, it was in the middle, like today. Seawater inundated the land because of a combination of continental warping and a global rise in sea level. Resistance to the tectonic forces moving the continent westward caused a down-warping of the land, forcing the continent's interior to buckle like

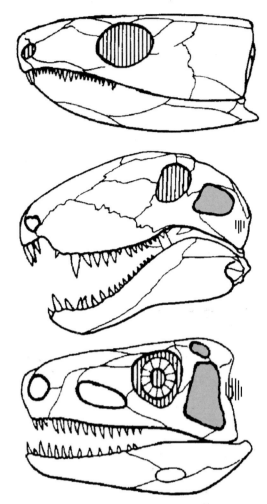

Figure 7. Vertebrate animals that have a reproductive system not dependent upon laying eggs in water are termed amniotes. This includes the reptiles, turtles, birds, and mammals.

The amniotes are divided into subgroups based on the number of openings in the skull behind the eye. The openings are shaded gray in the figure. The orbits and nasal openings are striped. Figures are not to scale.

Animals with no openings (top) are classed as **anapsids** *and are considered to be most primitive. Modern turtles are placed in this group.*

Then there developed a group whose skulls had a single opening (middle), called the **synapsids**. *This group consists of the mammal-like reptiles and includes the ancestors of mammals.*

Late in the Pennsylvanian Period, another group (bottom) evolved from anapsid stock to form the **diapsid** *group. This group contains the dinosaurs, pterosaurs, and all living reptiles.*

Figure 8. Below is a map of North America showing the areas covered by the sea in the Late Cretaceous. The exact boundaries are not all precisely known, and the coasts migrated back and forth over time as the sea encroached and retreated from the continental interior.

The location of Kansas is shown and it can be seen that most of the state was under water during that time. The mud and sediment at the bottom of the sea became the chalk and shale exposed in western Kansas today.

a carpet being pushed across a floor. The water that covered the center of the continent is considered to have been a shallow sea, not a true ocean.

Within the shallow sea of the Late Cretaceous, sediments were deposited in layers throughout the mid-continent. The layers record about 35 million years of history, from the early encroachment of the water about 100 million years ago almost until its final withdrawl at the end of the Cretaceous, 65 million years ago.

Western Kansas Rocks

Just as geologists give names to periods of time for effective communication, they also name the rock layers. For our purposes, the category of rock layer that will be most important is the formation. A formation is a formally named package of rock that is generally easy to distinguish from over- and under-lying layers. Figure 9 presents the formations that are exposed at the surface in western Kansas.

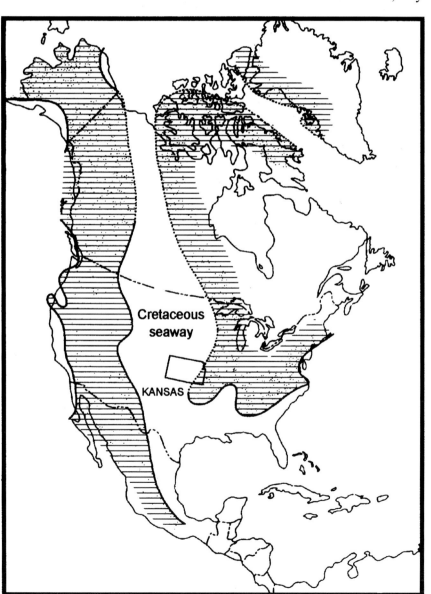

Cretaceous seaway

KANSAS

Figure 9. At right is a chart of the rocks exposed at the surface in western Kansas. The dashed lines represent breaks in the rock record, times of erosion or non-deposition. The dotted line at the bottom indicates where the rocks at the surface end. Numbers are in millions of years before the present (Ma).

Era	Period	Ma	Epochs/Stages	Rock-Stratigraphic Units		
Cenozoic	Quaternary	1.6	Pleistocene	Dune sand, alluvium, gravel, loess		
	Tertiary	10–5	Miocene	Ogallala Group		
Mesozoic	Late Cretaceous		Campanian	Pierre Shale	Weskan Shale	
					Sharon Springs	
		84		Niobrara Formation	Smoky Hill Chalk	
		87.5	Santonian			
		88.5	Coniacian		Fort Hays Limestone	
			Turonian	Carlile Shale	Codell Sandstone	
					Blue Hill Shale	
					Fairport Chalk	
		91		Greenhorn Formation	Pfeifer Shale	
					Jetmore Chalk	
			Cenomanian		Hartland Shale	
					Lincoln Limestone	
				Graneros Shale		
		97.5		Dakota Formation		
	Early Cretaceous		Albian	Kiowa Shale/Cheyenne Sandstone		

Figure 10. George Sternberg excavates elephant legs in western Kansas. These legs were found upright in the sediment, indicating that the animal died while mired in mud.

Chapter 3
The Birth of Palontology and Evolutionary Theory

Foundations of a Science

The science of paleontology is still very young compared to most of the other physical sciences. It is a hybrid science: part geology (the study of the earth) and part biology (the study of life). It did not really get started until the end of the eighteenth century, making the science about as old as the United States. The Enlightenment thinkers who became the founding fathers of this country were influenced by the newly developed modern scientific approach to solving questions about the world. One man, as vice president of the United States, published (in 1797) one of the first technical papers on prehistoric beasts in North America. That man was Thomas Jefferson.

Jefferson's paper was titled "A Memoir on the Discovery of Certain Bones of a Quadruped of the Clawed Kind in the Western Part of Virginia," and he described three large claws found in a Virginia cave. Jefferson named the beast *Megalonyx,* from the Greek roots of *mega* meaning large and *onyx* meaning claw. Jefferson thought that his giant clawed beast must have been a vicious carnivore.

Paleontology was a budding science 200 years ago. Little was understood about Earth's past and its prehistoric inhabitants. Indeed, it was not so long before Jefferson wrote his paper that modern western science had first come to understand that fossils did in fact represent evidence of living organisms. The term fossil comes from the Latin root *fossilis*, meaning literally to dig up, and the word originally was applied to anything dug from the ground, including what we now consider organic remains as well as rocks, minerals, and other curiosities.

By Enlightenment times of the eighteenth century, the term "fossil" had come to mean "the remains of organisms," but few studies had been made on them. In 1767, Benjamin

Figure 11. Machinery operators discovered this mastodon skull fragment in a sand pit in Kiowa County, Kansas. Mammoth and mastodon remains were important in proving that animals did become extinct. This head is lying upside down. The bumps of the teeth can be seen on the top right edge of the fossil. The knob on the top left is where the head attached to the neck.

By Enlightenment times of the eighteenth century, the term "fossil" had come to mean "the remains of organisms," but few studies had been made on them. In 1767, Benjamin Franklin reviewed some mastodon material sent to him when he was in London. He marveled that elephant remains could be found in North America and wrote, "They are extremely curious on many accounts; no living elephants having been seen in any part of America by any of the Europeans settled there, or remembered in any tradition of the Indians."

Extinction

Mastodon (fig. 11) and mammoth specimens found in the eastern United States received most of the attention from the scientific establishment in the late eighteenth century. Teeth and bones were found regularly in the beds of rivers, and they attracted attention perhaps because their large size was so different from the animals known to wander the forests at that time. There were many fanciful interpretations of the animals to which the remains belonged. One author, George Turner, speculated (in 1799) that the mastodon was "partly (if not wholly) carnivorous" in diet. "May it not be inferred, too, that as the largest and swiftest quadrupeds were appointed for his food, he necessarily was endowed with great strength and activity?—that, as the immense volume of the creature would unfit him for coursing after his prey through tickets and woods, Nature had furnished him with the power of taking it by a mighty leap?"

The Frenchman Georges Cuvier is credited with publishing the first modern paleontologic study in 1812, when he described the fossils of the Paris Basin in France. Cuvier was best known as an anatomist, and he studied the form of modern animals in great detail. With his skill at interpreting animal remains, he was able to accurately recreate the animals of the distant past and show how they were similar to and different from the modern forms. Cuvier's great contribution to science was his realization that the fossil animals he studied, although similar in many ways to modern animals, could not be found among the living animals of the world. Cuvier had found solid evidence for extinction.

Extinction of species was not something that fit into the worldview of the Enlightenment. Thomas Jefferson, very much an Enlightenment follower, gave clear instructions to the leaders of his western expedition, Lewis and Clark, to look for the *Megalonyx* among the carnivores of the west. If the remains of the giant claw were found in Virginia, surely it should be walking around in the wilds of the frontier. The Enlightenment thinkers had a concept called the Chain of Being, in which every living thing is viewed as connected as in a chain, from the lowest life form to the highest, which is man. But, so the argument went, just like a physical chain, the Chain of Being is only as strong as the weakest link, and should any link become lost, the entire chain would collapse. The Chain of Being has overtones of what we might consider the modern science of ecology, with the linking and interdependency of all living things within the environment. But the requirement that nothing can ever be removed from the environment, or become extinct, limited their view of the earth's past. If nothing can change, nothing can evolve.

George Turner, despite providing such fanciful speculation about the habits of the mastodon, correctly argued for the complete extinction of the group. "The benevolent persuasion, that no link in the chain of creation will ever be suffered to perish, has induced certain authors of distinguished merity, to provide a residence for our [mastodon] in the remote regions of the north." Turner even speculated on a cause for the disappearance of the great beast: "With the agility and ferocity of the tiger; with a body of unequalled magnitude and strength, it is possible that [mastodons] may have been at once the terror of the forest and of man!—And may not the human race have made the extirpation of this terrific disturber a common cause?"

Cuvier, with his careful observation and detailed anatomical work, added the nails to the coffin for arguments against extinction. Yes, whole groups of life forms did indeed vanish from the face of the earth. This led to the realization for the first time that the earth has not always looked as it does today, and that long-lost worlds populated by fantastic wild beasts were a reality.

Cuvier had a different explanation than Turner for how those extinctions could come about. He reasoned that the earth had undergone dramatic and sudden changes in climate and environment, and that these changes drove life forms over the edge into extinction. This worldview of major and dramatic change inducing extinction was later named catastrophism, although Cuvier preferred to call the events revolutions. In Cuvier's view, events of an unknown, and perhaps unknowable, origin served to "wipe the slate clean" as it were, and caused major turnovers in the life forms preserved in the rock record. The strict catastrophist view was contradicted by field observations, however. Cuvier only envisioned a half dozen or so catastrophic events and major faunal periods, but soon newly discovered fossils indicated that there were many more periods of life history. Something else was needed to explain the increasingly complex picture of earth history that was being revealed in the fossil record.

Deep Time & the Origin of Species

Charles Lyell, an Englishman, championed a new view of geologic history that came to be known as uniformitarianism. In contrast to catastrophism, uniformitarianism held that the processes still observable today were also responsible for changes that earth experienced in the past. This is a more scientific concept in that it does not rely on processes that are unknowable, as were Cuvier's revolutions. In the uniformitarian view, geologic processes happen continually, rather than catastrophic events. Rivers can be seen to cut into their banks, transporting sediments to the oceans; and the oceans move sand along the beach. Sediment accumulates in some areas and is stripped away in others. Over time, the face of the earth changes, not all at once, but gradually.

This approach had a corollary: if processes work gradually, then a great deal of time must be allowed to account for the observed changes in the land and animal life. Uniformitarianism does not shrink from this problem. The question of the age of the earth was one that had vexed scientists for some time. James Hutton (1726-1797) summed up the uniformitarin view of geologic time in one of the most famous lines in the entire geologic lexicon: "We find no vestige of a beginning, and no prospect of an end."

Charles Darwin was interested in the question of the origin of new life forms. Among the works that Darwin took with him for reference when he set sail on the *H.M.S. Beagle* in 1831 was Charles Lyell's *Principles of Geology*. Indeed, Darwin dedicated the second edition of his book *The Voyage of the Beagle* to Charles Lyell. Lyell's ideas of deep geologic time and Darwin's own observations while traveling the world on the *Beagle*

Figure 12. George F. Sternberg wraps plaster-soaked burlap around a fossil on one of his many collecting expeditions.

gave Darwin the seeds of his tremendously important work on evolution.

Darwin was a man who preferred to work quitely at home. He knew that the theory, which he put off publishing for almost three decades, would upset the scientific establishment, and he did not relish such an event. In fact, Darwin might never have published his ideas at all had another man not gotten a fever.

Alfred Russell Wallace was a naturalist collecting birds and insects in Southeast Asia. He, too, had been concerned with the development of new species, although not for as long as Darwin. Wallace described what happened to him:

"At that time [February 1858] I was suffering from a rather severe attack of intermittent fever at Ternate in the Moluccas...there suddenly flashed upon me the *idea* of the survival of the fittest—that the individuals removed by these checks must be on the whole inferior to those that survived. In the two hours that elapsed before my ague fit was over I had thought out almost the whole of the theory, and the same evening I sketched the draft of my paper, and in the two succeeding evenings wrote it out in full, and sent it by the next post to Mr. Darwin."

As might be expected, Darwin was taken aback. He had been working on this question for decades, carefully compiling evidence to support his theory, and here out of the blue another naturalist sent him a manuscript to review of his own ideas!

Darwin's friends convinced Wallace to co-author with him a paper to be given to the Linnaean Society outlining their ideas. Wallace graciously agreed that the older naturalist had much more empirical evidence gathered over years of research, and they jointly presented a short paper. Darwin worked hard to get the whole of his work published now that the cat was out of the bag, and in 1859 he published *The Origin of Species by Means of Natural Selection*. The impact of Darwin's work on the social and scientific communities has proven to be profound. In the coming years, Kansas would play a role in providing support for Darwin's important ideas.

Figure 13. George Sternberg (right) and a helper collect a fish skull in the Kansas chalk.

Figure 14. *In the past, as now, people enjoyed picnicing in the dramatic setting of the western Kansas chalk beds. Undated photograph by George Sternberg.*

Figure 15. Charles H. Sternberg in an
undated photograph.

Chapter 4
Geographic and Scientific Frontiers

The Early West

Darwin's book rocked the world, but the United States was absorbed with other concerns. The basic fabric of the country was being stretched with arguments about states' rights and the rights of humans. The culmination of this struggle was, of course, the Civil War, which threatened to tear apart the young nation. Science was turned to other matters, like inventing better weapons and healing those injured in battle.

At this point an army surgeon enters our story. George Miller Sternberg (1833–1915) was the oldest son of Levi and Margaret Sternberg. George M. served in the war, seeing firsthand the suffering caused by both the war and the crude medical practices of the day. Eventually, he would rise to the highest medical-military office in the country and serve as the Surgeon General of the United States. After the war, George M. was stationed at Fort Harker, near the town of Ellsworth, Kansas, and he encouraged his father to come to Kansas to help him manage a farm near the fort. So, in 1867, Levi Sternberg moved with his wife and the eight children still at home to the prairies of Kansas, still a rough frontier. One of the children still living with his parents was George M.'s younger brother, Charles H. Sternberg (1850–1943).

Charles had become interested in fossils as a young boy in his home state of New York, and coming to the open grasslands was an exciting opportunity for the youth. All around Fort Harker were hills of sandstone outcrops. These beautiful maroon, purple, and blood-red hills contained the fossils of ancient plants, leaves mostly, which Charles soon began to collect. The closest thing to a scientist that existed in most frontier areas was the doctor, so Charles brought his finds to the attention of his older brother, George Miller. George M., who was politically well-connected, had the leaves sent back to the Smithsonian Institution in Washington D.C. A letter

Figure 16. *Othniel C. Marsh.*

from that institution in response to the fossils sent did much to solidify Charles' ambition to become a fossil collector.

The next decade was a pivotal one for both Charles Sternberg the fossil hunter and the discipline of paleontology itself. And Kansas played a starring role in several ways. It was Charles' home-base for his fossil collecting expeditions and his specimen preparation laboratory. Two other giants of North American paleontology, Othniel C. Marsh and Edward Drinker Cope, began to recognize the prolific resources of the Kansas fossil beds. And those fossil beds began to yield a series of specimens that offered dramatic support for Darwin's newly published theory of natural selection.

The Early Kansas Connection

In 1870, with much fanfare, Othniel C. Marsh (fig. 16), a professor of Yale College, led one of the first scientific expeditions to the west. Marsh was the wealthy nephew of George Peabody and was himself politically connected. Marsh arranged for military escort and assistance through the frontier, and he recruited a field crew from the ranks of the Yale student body. These assistants had little interest in science (a plus for Marsh as he did not intend to share the scientific glory) and, probably most importantly, could fund their own way west.

His first excursion to the West was expedited by the new railroad system and, in contrast to the way earlier explorers had traveled, Marsh and his crew rode in relative comfort along the rails of the Union Pacific across Nebraska. They stopped in North Platte to pick up their military escort and Indian guides, and worked their way west into the fossil-rich badlands of western Nebraska. Buffalo Bill briefly accompanied them. Even though it was for only one day, Marsh later would brag a great deal about his time with the famed guide. If nothing else, Marsh knew a good opportunity to promote himself when he saw one. The journey was documented for the public by one of the graduate students, Charles Betts, who published accounts of the trip in *Harper's Magazine*:

Figure 17. Members of the Yale Expedition of 1872 pose for this studio photograph. Marsh (center back) and his crew collected many exciting fossils that year in Kansas including a complete skeleton of the toothed bird Hesperornis regalis.

"The guides rode about a mile in advance of the column. The major pointed out the least difficult paths; while the Indians, with movements characteristic of their wary race, crept up each high bluff, and from behind a bunch of grass peered over the top for signs of hostile savages. Next in line of march came the company of cavalry…and with them rode the Yale party, mounted on Indian ponies, and armed with rifle, revolver, geological hammer, and bowie-knife. Six army wagons, loaded with provisions, forage, tents, and ammunition, and accompanied by a small guard of soldiers, formed the rear."

The party headed westward into Wyoming and rested a few days in Salt Lake City, Utah. They continued west to San Francisco and returned to collect in the Green River Basin of southern Wyoming. They then turned south to the Smoky Hill River of western Kansas and got their first view of the Niobrara Formation. Marsh did not remain long in the Smoky Hill area, but he did make a fantastic discovery. One evening, while riding his pony back to camp along a bison trail, he spied a bone.

Although it was getting dark, Marsh jumped from the saddle and spent some time excavating it. His escort was getting nervous at the lateness of the hour, but Marsh paid no attention as he continued digging. It was an unusual bone, not quite like anything he had collected to date, and he carefully packed it for the trip home. He marked the rocks in the area of the find so that he could return in the future to look for more.

Marsh collected many fossils on that trip, but he was particularly interested in the strange bone from Kansas. He knew it to be a finger bone of some sort and that it was thin-walled and hollow. After careful study he concluded that it must belong to a pterodactyl, but the only ones known at that time were from Europe, and were considerably smaller than the specimen from Kansas. "The only joint much like it that I could find, in any animal, living or extinct, was in the wing finger of the Pterodactyl, or flying dragon."

Marsh calculated that the Kansas animal, with a 20 foot wingspan, was larger than anything from Europe. "Believing in my science, as taught by Cuvier, I determined to make a scientific announcement of what the fossil indicated and trust to future discoveries to prove whether I was right or wrong."

In 1871, Marsh again made a trip to Kansas, this time specifically to find more of his pterodactyl and toothed birds. Retracing his steps to the place where he marked the rock the year before, Marsh soon found more of the same animal. He traced out the bones as they came to light, and one by one he measured them as he took them up. On the spot, Marsh had proven his own, seemingly unbelievable, estimates on the size of the great flying dragon.

Thomas Henry Huxley: Darwin's Bulldog

During the many collecting trips that Marsh led or funded, he had his collectors focus their efforts on collecting fossil horses from as many geologic ages as possible. After careful study, Marsh was able to show how horses evolved from an early small, many-toed animal, to the large, single-toed form of today. The most preeminent scientist in the world at that time was Thomas Henry Huxley from the Royal School of Mines and the British Geological Survey. Huxley was the world's expert on fossil horses of the Old World and was such a staunch supporter of Darwin's new theory that he was awarded the nickname "Darwin's Bulldog." In 1876, Huxley made a trip to the New World. He wanted to see for himself some of the fantastic fossils he kept hearing about from the American West. Marsh was prepared for his distinguished guest, and had assistants trot out all the marvelous collection he had amassed.

Huxley was most impressed with Marsh's collection of fossil horses. Marsh could lay out 60 million years of horse evolution, from the small dog-sized animals of the early Cenozoic to the modern genus *Equus*. Huxley had assumed that horses evolved in the Old World, and it was common knowledge that, before the Spanish brought them to the New World, there were no living horses on those continents. However, slowly, with the overwhelming evidence Marsh produced for him, Huxley was beginning to see that the horse evolved in the New World and migrated to the Old World; not at all what he had thought before. As they talked, Huxley asked questions and Marsh called to his assistants to bring such-and-such specimen to illustrate some point. In the face of Marsh's fossil material, Huxley exclaimed "I

Figure 18. This illustration was doodled by Thomas Henry Huxley while visiting with Marsh and discussing horse evolution. Eohippus *was Huxley's jocular name for a horse he imagined to be waiting to be found in the American West. This fictitious, small, five-toed animal was surmised to be the ancestor of the modern horse. The primitive jockey was dubbed* Eohomo *to represent the earliest human. When Marsh found a horse ancestor that was similar, he named it* Eohippus *in honor of Huxley's cartoon.*

believe you are a magician. Whatever I want, you just conjure up."

Marsh told Huxley that somewhere in the West was an even older, more primitive species of horse waiting to be found. Huxley doodled what the primitive horse might have looked like with five toes and dubbed it *Eohippus*, or dawn horse. After Huxley left America, Marsh wrote him saying that the surmised primitive horse did exist and had been in an unopened crate that had been delivered to Marsh before Huxley came. They had been sitting within feet of the new beast! Marsh named it *Eohippus*, Huxley's jocular name for the "fictitious" animal (fig. 18).

Hen's Teeth: Birds With a Bite

Another important feather in Marsh's scientific cap was his work on the unusual Cretaceous toothed birds from

Figure 19. *Like his father Charles before him, George Sternberg collects leaf nodules near Carnerio in Ellsworth County, Kansas in 1927.*

Kansas. Darwin had published his earth-shaking book *The Origin of Species* just 20 years before. One of the seeming weaknesses of Darwin's hypothesis was the lack of fossil intermediaries between species end-points. If one species could transform into another over time by the gradual development of advantageous characters, as Darwin had suggested, some people argued that there should be a continuous chain of fossils displaying a series of character states. Darwin recognized that there was a lack of such evidence in the fossil record as known at that time, and he could only suggest that the fossil record was just too incomplete.

Soon after Darwin published, one dramatic example of a fossil intermediary was found in Germany. This was the famed *Archaeopteryx* (fig. 20), an animal with characters of both the ancestral reptile and the descendant bird rolled into one. On his 1871 expedition to the West, Marsh had found the headless skeleton of a six-foot long, flightless bird which he named *Hesperornis regalis* in a paper in 1872. Later in 1872, Marsh recieved a box of fossils from Benjamin Mudge of the Kansas Agricultural College in Manhattan. That box contained fossils of another bird that Marsh named *Ichthyornis*. In 1873 a specimen of *Hesperornis* was found with a head, and it amazed the scientific establishment because it possessed teeth, another fine fossil intermediary from the reptiles to the birds.

Marsh was to gain the most fame of his career when, in 1880, he published his large work on the fossil birds of the country, and he based his work on one hundred twenty-five individulas from Kansas. With *Archaeopteryx* and the Kansas birds in hand, Marsh dramatically proclaimed a victory for evolution in a lecture given in 1887 to the American Association for the Advancement of Science:

"The classes of Birds and Reptiles, as now living, are separated by a gulf so profound that a few years since it was cited by the opponents of evolution as the most important break in the animals series, and one that doctrine could not bridge over. Since then, as Huxley has clearly shown, this gap has been virtually filled by the discovery of bird-like Reptiles and reptilian Birds. *Compsognathus* and *Archaeopteryx* of the Old World, and *Ichthyornis* and *Hesperornis* of the new, are the stepping stones by which the evolutionist of today leads the doubting brother across the shallow remnant of the gulf, once thought impassable."

Kansas fossils offered dramatic support for the theory of evolution, and played an important role in the establishment of paleontology as a respected science. For the first time in scientific history, American scientists pulled ahead of their European conterparts in terms of their contributions to a field. Paleontology, like other uniquely American traits, came into its own in the American West.

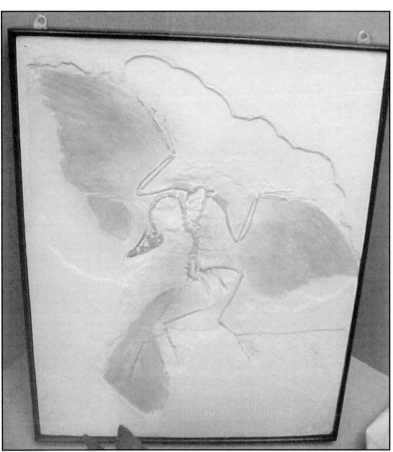

Figure 20. Archaeopteryx *was the first primitive bird discovered. Found in Jurassic rocks in Germany, it shares many features with dinosaurs, but the fossil shows that its feathers were developed well enough to allow for full flying capabilities.*

Figure 21. Edward Drinker Cope. Cope was Marsh's scientific rival and they struggled with each other for dominance of North American paleontology. Cope was first to employ Charles H. Sternberg as a fossil collector.

Sternberg Goes to the Field

Marsh was not the only scientist interested in the fossil fields of Kansas. His scientific rival, Edward D. Cope (fig. 21), also saw the value of getting into the field and making dramatic discoveries.

It was into this climate of scientific rivalry that Charles Sternberg came of age. In 1875 and 1876, Charles spent his only year as a student of higher education at Kansas State Agricultural College. He was eager to join a collecting party into the West, and quite disappointed when he was unable to join a party organized by Professor B. F. Mudge, who was going to collect for Marsh. Sternberg later wrote in his autobiography:

"I made every effort in my power to secure a place in the party, but failed, as it was full when I applied. It has always been hard, however, for me to give up what I have determined to accomplish; so, although almost with despair, I turned for help to Professor E. D. Cope, of Philadelphia, who was becoming so well known that a report of his fame had reached me at Manhattan.

"I put my soul into the letter I wrote him, for this was my last chance. I told him of my love for science, and of my earnest longing to enter the chalk of western Kansas and make a collection of its wonderful fossils, no matter what it might cost me in discomfort and danger. I said, however, that I was too poor to go at my own expense, and asked him to send me three hundred dollars to buy a team of ponies, a wagon, and a camp outfit and to hire a cook and driver. I sent no recommendations from well-known men as to my honesty or executive ability, mentioning only my work in the Dakota Group.

"I was in a terrible state of suspense when I had despatched [sic] the letter, but fortunately, the Professor responded promptly, and when I opened the envelope, a draft for three hundred dollars fell at my feet. The note which accompanied it said: 'I like the style of your letter. Enclose draft. Go to work,' or words to the same effect.

"That letter bound me to Cope for four long years, and enabled me to endure immeasurable hardships and privations in the barren fossil fields of the West; and it has always been one of the joys of my life to have known intimately in field and shop the greatest naturalist America has produced."

Sternberg had finally begun what would be a long career, throughout which he did indeed suffer many "hardships and privations." The hard labor did not deter him, even in that first year. He wrote:

"The incessant labor, however, had a weakening effect upon my system so that I fell a victim to malaria, and when a violent attack of shaking ague came on, I felt as if fate were indeed against me.

"I remember how, one day, when I was in the midst of a shaking fit, I found a beautiful specimen of a Kansas mosasaur. *Clidastes tortor* Cope named it, because an additional set of articulations in the backbone enabled it to coil. Its head lay in the center, with the column around it, and the four paddles stretched out on either side. It was covered by only a few inches of disintegrated chalk.

Figure 22. Levi Sternberg (foreground) works on a duck-billed (hadrosaurian) dinosaur skeleton.

"Forgetting my sickness, I shouted to the surrounding wilderness, 'Thank God! Thank God!' And I did well to thank the Creator, as I slowly brushed away the powdered chalk and revealed the beauties of this reptile of the Age of Reptiles."

In the years to come, Sternberg would marry and have several children. The oldest boy would be named George Fryer, his first name given in honor of Charles' older brother. All his sons, George, Charles M, and Levi, would form the core of a family fossil collecting operation. For the next 75 years, the name "Sternberg" would ring loudly in the halls of fossil museums around the world.

Figure 23. Before the Sternbergs started collecting dinosaurs, only 13 Triceratops *skulls were known. After just a few years the Sternbergs added another 6 skulls.*

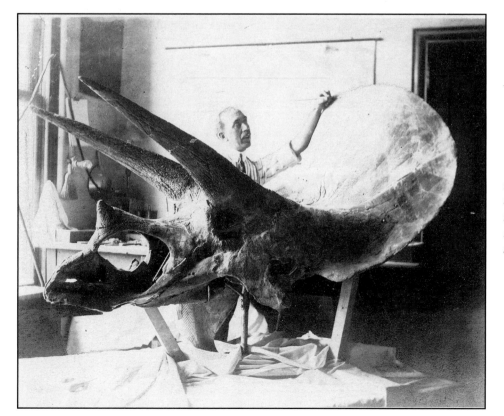

Figure 24. The same skull shown above being mounted at the American Museum of Natural History in New York City.

Chapter 5
Hooray for Hadrosaurs

Sternbergs go to Canada, and Dinosaurs!

Charles H. Sternberg and his three sons, George F., Charles M., and Levi, moved north to Canada in 1916 to continue collecting in rich fossil fields. In the opening of his second autobiography, Charles H. Sternberg seems amazed that life in Canada was not dictatorial.

"Think of it! After three years' [sic] of residence in the beautiful city of Ottawa, the capital of all the broad expanse north of the international line, after four seasons of work among buried dinosaurs and three winters spent in the laboratory of the Victoria Memorial Museum of Ottawa, I am free to confess I would not have known so far as personal liberty was concerned, that I was all this time in the employ of his Royal Majesty George the Fifth of England and ruler of the British Empire. I have learned, I believe, that a man is as much a man amidst the snows of the Lady of the North, under the Union Jack, as under my own beloved Stars and Stripes. Our hopes, our ideals, our aims are much the same."

The Dinosaur Mummy & Early Success

Several years prior to moving north, the Sternbergs continued to make their reputations collecting in the American West, in South Dakota and Wyoming. In 1908, George F. made the first of what he counted as the three most important fossil discoveries of his career, the dinosaur mummy (fig. 25). The specimen was a duck-billed dinosaur (hadrosaur) preserved in its contorted death pose, with the entombing sand preserving impressions and casts of skin, muscles, and some of its internal organs. The animal must have died in a relatively dry place and desiccated soon after death. The drying contorted the body into a grotesque pose. Soon after, sand was deposited over the carcass, filling in the body cavities and pressing against the skin to preserve minute details of skin texture. This is as close as science can come to finding a frozen dinosaur. The Sternbergs considered it one of the greatest discoveries of their career. Today, the dinosaur mummy is on display at the American Museum of Natural History in New York City in the recently remodeled Dinosaur Hall.

The Sternbergs continued this success of their first years of the century by collecting many *Triceratops* skulls and additional hadrosaur material with skin impressions. Thirteen *Triceratops* skulls were known prior to their 1908–1910 work. After their fruitful collecting, the Sternbergs single-handedly added another six *Triceratops* skulls and two nearly complete hadrosaurs, both with preserved skin impressions.

A Bone Hunter's Work is Never Done

Figure 25. At the right is a picture of the dinosaur mummy found by George Sternberg in 1908 and collected by him and his brother and father. This specimen was the first of what George considered to be the three highlights of his career. It is now on display at the American Museum of Natural History in New York City.

Charles H. wrote of the intense labor required to move some of the large blocks of rock containing the hadrosaur:

"Owing to the great size of the specimen, and as I was determined to save every particle of the skin, the sections we took up were very heavy, especially those composing the trunk, one of which weighed about 3,500 pounds. It took considerable skill and the combined strength of the four of us to handle these huge masses of rock and bone, especially as we had no tackle. We learned, however, that with a couple of cottonwood poles for levers and blocks of the same for fulcrums, we could hoist a section up, and then while the boys held it a few inches above the ground, I would shovel sand under it and tamp it with my shovel handle. Of course, when they loosened their hold to take a new bite, it sank deeply into the sand again, but still we found we had gained an inch or two. Working thus all day we not only raised a section weighing 3,500 pounds four feet in the air, but moved it several feet to one side, so we could run the wagon under it and load."

Hadrosaur Crests

The hadrosaur specimen that Sternberg referred to above was a non-crested hadrosaur. As this implies, there were also crested hadrosaurs, with bony protrusions from their heads forming a wide variety of shapes. The family of fossil

Figure 26. *Many times the Sternbergs needed to move large slabs of wrapped fossils. A horse-drawn sled was used to bring the huge bundles to camp where shipping crates were made. A hoist eased the job of packing the heavy crates.*

hunters collected several important crested hadrosaur specimens in Canada. One was a nearly complete skeleton of *Corythosaurus*. This large animal was so named because its crest resembled the crest on a Corinthian helmet. In the third floor diorama of the Sternberg Museum we modeled a *Corythosaurus* adult male and a juvenile moving with a herd across river floodplain.

Several different sizes of crests have been found among the hadrosaurs. There are a variety of interpretations for this. One is that the different-sized crests represent separate species. In the species-naming free-for-all that existed in days gone by, they were all given separate names. However, recent examination suggests an alternative hypothesis. Perhaps the different-sized crests on these very similar animals represent variation within one species, showing large and small, young and adult, and male and female forms. With this thought in mind, many old species have been regrouped into *Corythosaurus*, and we are beginning to look at the animals as individuals within a population that shows a range morphology.

In this view, the males may have displayed the larger crests. Display for attracting mates and intimidating potential rivals is common in the animal kingdom. For this reason, our modeled *Corythosaurus* is a "he." His crest is bold, projecting to the front. Although we did not restore it this way, the crest may have been brightly colored, especially during the breeding season. The *Corythosaurus* in the foreground of the mural is a female. Her crest is slightly reduced and does not project as prominently towards the front.

Both crested and non-crested hadrosaurs are shown mingling in the herd that wanders across the river flood plain. In hadrosaurs, the nasal openings at the end of the snout connect to the sinus passageways of the head, which run through the crest (if present), behind the eyes, and down into the throat to the lungs. There were a wide variety of crest shapes. Much speculation has been given as to the function of the crests, focusing on the connection of the lungs and nasal passageways through the crest. Some of the suggestions include that the crests served as snorkels to be used when the animal wandered around swamps with its head submerged, or that the crests were air storage chambers to be used like modern-day scuba diving air tanks, so the animal could stay underwater longer. However, the volume of the crest is not nearly as large as the lungs, and it is unlikely that there would have been enough air to sustain the oxygen needs of the animal.

More recently, researchers have suggested that the connection with the lungs worked in reverse order, that is, to expel air through the nose, not just to suck it in. It has been shown that, if we think of the lungs as a large set of bellows that forces air out of the nasal passageways, the animal could have produced sound. Each differently shaped crest could have acted like the tubing of different musical instruments, giving each species of crested hadrosaur its own unique "call."

Of course, the ability to call implies the ability to respond and understand some limited communication between individuals of the same species. Thus, communication might imply some sort of community structure. There is strength in numbers and good reason for relatively large, defenseless herbivores to congregate together. There are more eyes to watch for danger, and less chance that any one individual will be singled out by a predator for dinner. The odds are further improved if individuals of more than one species can cooperate.

Cooperation like this would not work well if the two species directly competed for the same food source. So, perhaps one species preferred one kind of plant and a second favored another. Why not group together for mutual protection? The more eyes the better. In the upland mural there are several species shown together. The crested *Corythosaurus* is shown with the non-crested *Edmontosaurus*. There are even non-hadrosaurs in the group, including *Triceratops*, of which the Sternbergs had found so many near the turn of the century. This herding together of different species is no

Figure 27. A female Corythosaurus *moves with the herd across the flood plain in the museum's upland diorama.*

different than modern zebra and wildebeest herding together in the African savannas today.

One might imagine whole herds of bellowing hadrosaurs calling contentedly back and forth, each species with its own distinctive "horn" to blow the "all clear" signal to the group. But when danger does loom, the bellowing of the herd changes dramatically. Listen in the museum's upland diorama. When all is clear and safe, the bellowing animals are peaceful. But, when the *Tyrannosaurus* makes its presence known, pandemonium breaks out. The contented bellows become high-pitched squeals of excitement, warning of immediate danger. The herd reacts quickly and stampedes to safety, causing confusion in any pursuing carnivore by the continual shifting of individuals, making it difficult for the hunter to focus in on a single individual. There is indeed safety in numbers.

Figure 28. A mixed herd of Triceratops *and hadrosaurs keeps an eye out for danger while feeding in a river flood plain in the museum's upland diorama.*

Figure 29. *The non-crested hadrosaur* Edmontosaurus *is portrayed in the museum's upland diorama.*

Figure 30. *The Sternbergs collected from boats along the Red Deer River in Alberta, Canada and used the boats to transport their fossils out of the area. They collected many hadrosaurs, including both* Edmontosaurus *and* Corythosaurus.

Figure 31. *Levi Sternberg provides the scale for a photograph of dinosaur bones found in Converse County, Wyoming, in 1908.*

Chapter 6
Dinosaur Diorama: Meet the Cast

Dinosaurs of the Upland Diorama

So far in our story we have zoomed from the Late Mississippian to the wild West. Now, we return to prehistoic times, finding ourselves in the middle of the Age of Dinosaurs, in the Jurassic Period (208–144 million years ago). Long-necked dinosaurs, called sauropods, attained the largest size ever achieved by a land animal. There were many kinds of sauropods, and it seems that scientists try to outdo each other with the names: *Brontosaurus* (thunder dinosaur), *Brachiosaurus* (arm dinosaur), *Ultrasaurus* (ultimate dinosaur), *Seismosaurus* (earth shaker dinosaur), *Supersaurus* (super big dinosaur), and *My-saurus-is-bigger-than-your-saurus*. In any case, these animals were large. The sauropods had their heyday during the Jurassic, and by the Cretaceous Period we do not find as many, at least in North America. If you look at the hillside of the upland diorama you will find an outcrop representing the famous dinosaur bone beds of the Morrison Formation.

Today, the Morrison Formation is exposed throughout the Rocky Mountains from Montana to New Mexico. This unit

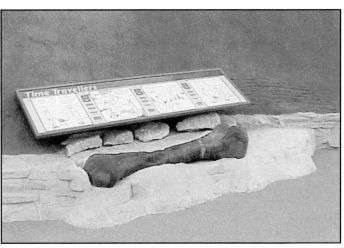

Figure 32. Contemporaries of the fierce Allosaurus *included many of the large, long-necked dinosaurs called sauropods. An actual femur, or thighbone, from an unidentified sauropod is exposed in a Morrison Formation outcrop depicted in the upland diorama. The Morrison Formation preserves many fossils of these behemoths of the past.*

Figure 33. The Jurassic predator Allosaurus *had been extinct for about 60 milllion years before the first* Tyrannosaurus *walked on the earth. That means about the same amount of time seperated these two dinosaurs as seperates us from* T. rex. *The museum's upland diorama depicts a cast of an* Allosaurus *skull in a Morrison Formation outcrop.*

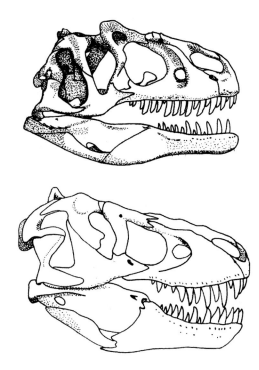

Figure 34. *Compare the profiles of the Jurassic* Allosaurus *on the top with the Cretaceous* Tyrannosaurus rex *on the bottom. The skulls are drawn to the same size, not to scale.*

Note that although both were obviously eating meat, they were built differently. The skull of T. rex *is much more heavily built. See how much thicker the lower jaw behind the last tooth of* T. rex *is compared to* Allosaurus. *The bones of* Tyrannosaurus *could withstand greater forces, and larger muscles attached to its jaws created larger bite forces than those of* Allosaurus.

preserves a diverse set of environments that existed across that region during the Jurassic Period and is world-famous for its dinosaur content. It was the Morrison Formation that attracted the early nineteenth century collectors to the mountainous West, and they amassed huge dinosaur collections; both the sizes and numbers of dinosaur bones were huge. Look in the hillside outcrop of our Morrison beds and you will find two of the most characteristic fossils from the Jurassic: a sauropod leg bone and an *Allosaurus* skull.

Allosaurus was one of the largest meat-eating dinosaurs until *T. rex*. In contrast to *Tyrannosaurus rex*, there is a relatively good fossil record of *Allosaurus* from the Morrison Formation. Over 44 individuals were found at the Cleveland-Lloyd Quarry in Utah alone. Some of the largest individuals reached about 40 feet long, almost as long as the Cretaceous *T. rex*. These Jurassic predators are thought to have hunted in packs, with their food of choice probably being the wide variety of long-necked dinosaurs from the same time.

The Tyrant Lizard King

In 1902, two unconnected events occurred that affect our story. The first was the founding of Fort Hays State University (FHSU), the parent institution of the Sternberg Museum of Natural History. Fort Hays State University was carved out of land once owned by the federal government and used as Fort Hays, a fort to protect the railroad workers and settlers in the Kansas prairie from 1867 to 1889. After the fort closed, and after much work by one Hays man in particular, Martin Allen, the old fort land was given to the people of Kansas to be used for three purposes. The federal government decreed that the land be used 1) to establish a western branch of the Kansas Agricultural College (Kansas State University Agricultural Research Center today); 2) to establish a western branch of the Kansas state normal institute (FHSU today); and 3) for a public park (Frontier Park today).

The other event of 1902 that is significant to the story of prehistoric life was the discovery of the most famous dinosaur of all time: *Tyrannosaurus rex*. Just the name conjures images in our brains. This is an animal of superlatives. The largest terrestrial meat-eater of all time, the animal with the strongest bite, the star of the Hollywood silver screen, and the animal with the funniest front legs. *Tyrannosaurus rex* is all of this and more. Amazingly, in the last 100 years only a handful of specimens with any degree of completeness have become known to science. Think about that: the dinosaur that we collectively know on sight is one of the least represented in the fossil record.

What do we really know about this animal? In some ways we know a great deal. From its skeleton we can see that it had a massive head (figs. 34 and 35). Its jaws were thick, its head wide, and its neck sturdy. All of this points to huge muscles to operate the bite mechanism, and in conjunction with spike-like teeth, the bite of this beast must have been the most awesome force to crush another living thing. The sturdy, thick, deeply anchored teeth must have been able to withstand tremendous crushing forces, and in turn, have been able to deliver bone-crushing wounds to its victims.

A hadrosaur skeleton excavated in 1977 near Drumheller, Canada, provides terrifing evidence of the destructive power of a *Tyrannosaurus*. The back half of the skeleton was exposed in the rock, and the excavators thought they had a complete animal. However, as they continued to expose the front part of the hadrosaur they began to notice isolated tyrannosaur teeth. The farther they went toward the front of the skeleton, the more tyrannosaur teeth they found, and the hadrosaur skeleton no longer consisted of whole bones, but instead became a mass of bone chips. One or more tyrannosaurs had crushed up the entire front half of the hadrosaur!

The hind legs and trunk of the *T. rex* were massive. It stood 15 feet high at the hips and was 40 feet long. Its head alone was 5 feet long. The weight of a live *T. rex* has been estimated to be about 10,000 to 16,000 pounds (5 to 8 tons). For comparison, an average bull African elephant weighs about 11,000 pounds.

We can measure the skeletal proportions of *T. rex*, but its lifestyle and aspects of its physiology are harder to get at from the fossil record. This leads to questions that have gotten a lot of attention in the popular press: Were dinosaurs "warm blooded" or "cold blooded" and was *T. rex* a scavenger or a true hunter?

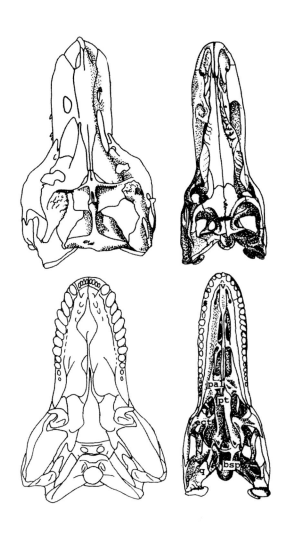

Figure 35. *Take another look at the* Tyrannosaurus rex *skull (left) compared to the* Allosaurus *skull (right). In the upper pair of skulls, you are above the dinosaurs looking straight down on their heads. Right away you can see that* T. rex *had a much wider head.*

In the lower figure, showing the roof of the mouth, note that the Allosaurus *has large openings in the bones of the roof of the mouth, whereas the* T. rex *has a more solid palate. This would have allowed* T. rex*'s skull to better withstand twisting movements. An attacking* T. rex *might have crushed its victim to death with its massive jaws and thick teeth, and then torn it apart with powerful twisting movements of its head and neck.*

Let's look at the question of metabolism. Can we tell if *T. rex*, or any of the dinosaurs, were "warm blooded?" We need to first define our terms so we are clear on what we are talking about. What is commonly called "warm blooded" usually refers to a particular set of conditions in an organism. These conditions imply that 1) the animal can keep its body temperature within a narrow range (called homeothermy); and 2) that the animal generates heat within its body to maintain that constant temperature (called endothermy). The opposite condition is poikilothermy, where the body temperature fluctuates with the environment. And ectothermy names the condition in which an organism cannot control body temperature metabolically but relies on the environment for temperature control.

Strictly speaking, an animal would not have to be endothermic to maintain homeothermy. For example, organisms that live in environments with little fluctuation in temperature can maintain their bodies at a constant temperature without exerting any energy to do so. They animal would be considered an ectothermic homeotherm.

People most often understand the metabolism debate to be one of ectothermy verses endothermy. When dinosaurs were first described it was apparent that their bone structure was very similar to modern-day reptiles. Richard Owen first coined the term "dinosaur" to try to describe these unique beasts. *Dino* comes from Greek meaning terrible, fearful, or awe-inspiring, and *sauros*, also from Greek, means lizard or reptile. So Owen's combination of these roots to form the term that we are familiar with describes those fearful "lizards" well.

However, many traits of the dinosaurs were similar to modern birds and mammals, and this suggested to some that while dinosaurs are unique, they might have some biological similarity to modern endotherms. Owen thought that some dinosaurs were more active, more energetic, and more bird-like in their physiology. However, subsequent workers impressed upon the popular psyche the impression of all dinosaurs as being sluggish behemoths confined to swamps. The term dinosaur came to mean anything that was out-dated, out-of-touch, and just plain too slow to adapt to the world. In the dinosaur revolution of the last several decades, Owen's original ideas have been gaining a wider acceptance and it now seems that the real-life dinosaurs were anything but sluggish, overgrown lizards.

Dinosaur Metabolism 1: Stance

One of the first things to notice about dinosaurs is the way that they stood and held their bodies. Notice how the reconstructions in the museum hold their legs straight underneath the trunk, not sprawled out to the side like a modern crocodile or lizard. Dinosaur legs are directly beneath the body, allowing more efficient use of energy in locomotion. While walking, dinosaurs would not have swung their bodies side to side in wild arcs like a lizard. Rather, they walk with stately strides more like an elephant. One might suggest that these straight, pillar-like legs would have been necessary for the larger dinosaurs to hold up their weight against gravity. However, even the smallest dinosaurs show the upright pattern. More than

Figure 36. *George Sternberg stands next to a* Corythosaurus *skeleton he and his family collected. Date ca. 1930.*

Relationship of Volume to Surface Area

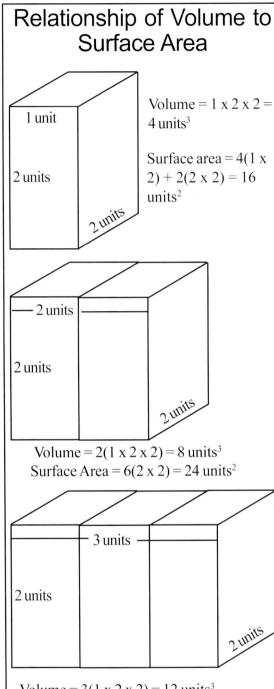

Volume = 1 x 2 x 2 = 4 units³

Surface area = 4(1 x 2) + 2(2 x 2) = 16 units²

Volume = 2(1 x 2 x 2) = 8 units³
Surface Area = 6(2 x 2) = 24 units²

Volume = 3(1 x 2 x 2) = 12 units³
Surface Area = 4(3 x 2) + 2(2 x 2) = 32 units²

Figure 37. Note that the volume grew from 4 to 12 units³ (3 times larger), while the suface area grew from 16 to 32 units² (only 2 times larger). Therefore, you can see that volume increases at a faster rate then surface area, and larger animals have proportionately less surface area.

just holding the animal against gravity, the benefit of this leg design would have been increased efficiency in walking and running.

Dinosaur Metabolism 2: Bone Growth Patterns

Bone growth patterns are another indication of the metabolic rates of dinosaurs. Bone is a living tissue inside an organism, not just a rigid, unbending framework for muscle attachments. Bones can record the growth of an individual somewhat like rings in trees. As an animal grows, new bone tissue forms and, at the microscopic level, the pattern of bone growth can be examined. Dinosaurs show a pattern of growth that is more similar to modern birds and mammals than it is to modern reptiles. Dinosaur bones show continuous growth during their juvenile years. Modern reptile bones show times of increased growth offset by times of slowed or no growth. This pattern represents the modern reptiles' metabolic response to fluctuations in food availability and seasonality: they "shut down" their growth for periods of time. The fact that dinosaurs do not show this indicates that they lived in environments with limited seasonality (which does seem to be the case from other lines of evidence) and/or they grew continually and quickly as juveniles, like modern birds and mammals do.

Dinosaur Metabolism 3: Ecological Arguments

The hazards of life are great, especially for the very young. We know that dinosaurs were egg-layers. There is, however, a limit to how large an egg can be. The embryo inside an egg must get its oxygen from the outside and must expel waste gas to the outside, so eggshell is permeable to gas. However, beyond a certain size, oxygen and waste cannot effectively pass through the egg to nourish the growing embryo. So, even the largest long-necked dinosaurs could only lay eggs that were many times smaller than the adult. This means that the young born to the largest of the dinosaurs were only a fraction of their adult size and weight. They needed to grow quickly in order to reach a size at which predators would no longer be a threat, and that means a fast growth curve. Birds and mammals today grow relatively quickly with their stepped-up metabolism. It would seem that, if dinosaurs could have achieved a similar metabolism, it would have been a great advantage.

It is possible that dinosaurs changed their metabolic pattern throughout their life times. They might have been endothermic while young and undergoing a great growing spurt, and then slowed their metabolism down somewhat after reaching adulthood. In fact, some of the truly giant dinosaurs may not have needed to generate much heat at all, but were able instead to keep their body chemistry moving along at a high pace due to their great bulk alone. This concept, called passive endothermy, is another point to consider.

It is a basic mathematic principle that the total surface area of a three-dimensional object grows slower than its mass (fig. 37). The effect of this relationship is that larger organisms have less surface area across which to dissipate heat than do smaller organisms. We can observe this in everyday life when the larger husband is too hot and the smaller wife is too cold (hormones can also control body temperature, in which case, this generalization does not always hold true). The husband has less surface area relative to mass to lose heat and retains it better than the wife. Large elephants don't need to worry about generating heat in the African plains. Rather, their large bodies collect heat from the environment and from their metabolism and they must getting rid of extra heat. Therefore, they fan themselves with their large ears, and their ears provide a lot of surface area to dissipate body heat through the numerous blood vessels close to the surface of the skin.

Likewise, very large dinosaurs may have been able to maintain their body heat just by being large. Once warmed up, it might have taken very little energy to keep the body warm and everything working at a mammal-like pace. This dinosaur would be considered an ectothermic homeotherm. The jury is still out on exactly how dinosaur metabolism worked, and I suspect we will find that they were doing different things at different times of their individual lives, and at different points in their evolution. Nature cannot so easily be pigeonholed.

Hunting King or Big Bully?

So, to address another question: was *T. rex* an active hunter, using high-voltage metabolism to be the fiercest carnivore ever, or was it predominately a scavenging bully? Again, the terms used in the popular media must be examined. What is the difference between a scavenger and hunter? It turns out this is not a black-and-white division in nature, but a man-made distinction. In reality, animals function on a continuum of behavior. My favorite example is the bears. Are bears, as a group, carnivorous predators, herbivorous, scavengers, or something else? The answer is, "Yes, they are all that."

Modern black bears tend to forage for insect grubs and eat a lot of vegetation, but they will eat carrion when they can. Grizzlies also eat carrion and have been known to kill large prey like moose, but they can get by on berries.

Figure 38. *How to kill a* Tyrannosaurus rex.

Polar bears are the closest example in the bear group to an obligate carnivore—they have to eat seals because there is little else to choose from in the Arctic. Even within a single bear species there is variation, with some individual grizzlies preferring to hunt instead of eating berries and some individuals just the opposite. Even among the most active hunters in the large mammal world, the big cats, there is no clear-cut division. All of the big cats will chase smaller carnivores off of their captured prey if that is easier than going out and killing their own dinner. Conservation of energy is the rule in modern, and past, ecosystems.

Another part of the puzzle is this: could *T. rex* run? If it hunted in a very active way we would expect that it ran well, or at least better than its prey. But, here again, the evidence is contradictory. Based on dinosaur trackway evidence it seems that the carnivorous dinosaurs walked most of the time. This is not surprising. Conservation of energy again: from trackway data, medium to large carnivorous dinosaurs walked about 5–10 km/h (about 3–6 mph), which is about the same as medium to large mammals. But this does not address running. Estimates have ranged from about 10–70 km/h (6–44 mph), but the higher estimates are controversial.

Consider what would happen to a *T. rex* running along at 35 mph if it tripped. A bipedal *T. rex* carries its chest and vital organs almost 10 feet above the ground, and its head is even higher. Without forelimbs able to catch the animal on the way down, the entire force of the massive body falling to the ground potentially would slam poor *T. rex's* head and chest into the ground, crushing its vital organs (fig. 38). It does not seem to me that running is an activity that they would engage in very often.

Figure 39. *George Sternberg holds an* Albertosaurus *jaw collected in Canada in about 1921.* Albertosaurus *was a close relative of* Tyrannosaurus.

Dinosaur Dung Beetles

In certain circles, dung is a valued commodity. Think about herds of herbivorous animals moving across a floodplain. They eat and defecate their way along. However, as hard as their digestive systems work to break down the plant material into components usable by their bodies, they are never perfectly efficient, and many nutrients are left behind in their droppings.

Figure 40. A dung beetle from South America.

One insect group has learned to take advantage of this resource: the dung beetles. These beetles, sometimes very colorful and some of them quite large, make their living by collecting dung. Some species make their burrows underneath a dung pile and feed from below, while others collect it and roll it into balls that they push back to a burrow. Eggs are laid on the nutrient-rich dung and the larva feed on the dung.

There is now evidence that dung beetles fed upon the dung of dinosaurs. A pile of re-worked dinosaur dung has been found in Montana, clear evidence that the dung beetle developed its unique taste preference on dinosaur droppings.

So, was *T. rex predominantly* a predator or a scavenger? The answer is that we still don't know, and it really does not matter. I seriously doubt that a *T. rex* would have passed up a chance to chase a few *Dromaeosaurus* off a kill that the smaller predators had just made. At the same time, I suspect that nothing was more formidable than a hungry *T. rex* lunging toward a juvenile *Corythosaurus*.

Tyrannosaurus Sex

What is the sex of the Sternberg Museum's *T. rex* model? You might hear staff members refer to the model as a female. Why is that? As with the *Corythosaurus* model, museum staff are using the diorama to suggest another tidbit of information about the natural world, knowing full well that we might be wrong. One study of *T. rex* suggested that there were two different size groups, one group slightly more slender than the other. In addition, the more robust forms seemed to have more space in the pelvic passageway. The space was created by the lack of a bony projection at the base of the tail, and this suggested that the more robust form was the one laying the eggs, and thus the female. We are all "mammal-centric," and we are used to the males of the species being the larger, stronger form. However, it is not unheard of (or even uncommon) in the animal kingdom for the female to be larger. For example, in owls, a predatory group of birds that are distant relatives of *T. rex*, the female is larger.

Recently, some questions have been raised about the reality of the differences in the pelvic structure between the two size-types. The most complete *T. rex* uncovered to date, popularly known as "Sue," is of the larger size type, and was thought to be a female on that basis. However, preparation of the specimen revealed that Sue does preserve the bony projection at the base of the tail. So the presence or absence of the bony projection and the overall size may not be an indication of sex, and we may in fact have "A boy named Sue."

Plants: Food for Thought

The Late Cretaceous was a period of great upheaval in the natural world. Mosasaurs and *Tyrannosaurus rex* inhabited a world of change that ultimately overturned the world of the giant reptiles. Similarly, plants were being affected in ways that forever influenced their evolution.

In the Early Cretaceous, angiosperm (flowering plants) pollen accounts for only 1% of the pollen preserved in the fossil record. The landscape was dominated by the gymnosperms (conifers and their relatives) and for almost 130 million years dinosaurs were adapted to life with the gymnosperms. However, by the end of the Cretaceous, flowering plant pollen made up to 70% of the plant fossil

Figure 41. Plants are near the base of the food chain. Most other life depends on them either for food, or to feed their prey.

A juvenile Corythosaurus *feeds on ferns as the herd ambles along.*

record. Flowers bloomed on the land while Kansas was the submerged home of giant lizards and fish.

One major advance of the flowering plants over their predecessors was a trend toward coevolution with animal pollinators. Gymnosperms rely primarily on the wind to carry their pollen to other plants for fertilization and to bring the pollen of other plants to them. A better system might be possible if plants could use animals to carry their pollen to others of the same species, exactly the strategy developed by the angiosperms.

Flowers are advertisements that are designed to attract animals, usually insects. Some flowers have developed elaborate mechanisms to entice insects to stop by, for example to feed on sweet nectar provided by the plant. But there is never a free lunch. While the insect is feasting, the anthers, or pollen-bearing organs of the plant, transfer pollen to the insect carrier. At the same time the insect visitor transfers pollen collected from previously visited plants and deposits it on the style of the pistil, or female organs of the plant. Pollen contains the sperm cells and these combine with the egg cell in the pistil during fertilization.

Along with increased probability of successful fertilization, the angiosperms went one step farther. They developed fruits to house the end-product of fertilization, seeds with their enclosed embryos. If the fruits are attractive to animals they will get picked up and eaten. The fruit provides some nutritional value to the animal, but more importantly for the plant, the animal passes the seeds through the gut, and deposits them in fecal piles. What better way to start out, than to be buried in a nutrient-rich deposit, ready to spring to life?

In the Late Cretaceous, flowering plants began to expand into new biologic niches. The animal life had to cope or face extinction. Insects thrived because they were ideal pollinators from the plants' perspective, and elaborate systems for mutual benefit evolved between plants and insects. The dinosaurs may not have fared so well, and the major change in the plant life is one reasonable explanation for declining dinosaur populations prior to the end of the Mesozoic.

The Sternberg Museum's upland diorama portrays representative plant life of the Late Cretaceous. The plants in the diorama were selected to represent major

Figure 42. Ferns and gymnosperms like cycads, conifers, and gingkos dominated the Mesozoic. Toward the end of the Mesozoic in the Cretaceous, flowering plants began to dominate the landscape.

plant groups, without modeling any specific fossil species. Toward the end of the Cretaceous, ferns, palms, ginkgo, and cycads, as well as plants with large flowers similar to *Magnolia*, have been found in the fossil record.

In fact, *Archaeanthus,* one of the best-preserved early flowers, comes from the Cretaceous Dakota Formation of western Kansas (fig. 43). Reconstructed from a number of separate parts (flower, leaves, stem, etc.) collected in close proximity and thought to reasonably be the same plant, it has a large, magnolia-like flower, a large fruiting body, and leaves that are unique in shape. More detailed studies based on actual fossil plants are needed to fully understand what the landscape of the Late Cretaceous was like. Such studies are currently in progress by staff of the Sternberg Museum.

So, during the Late Cretaceous, the plant life was beginning to look like what we are used to today, with the major exception that grass had not yet evolved. Today, grasses cover more than 30% of the Earth's land surface and provide more than half the calories consumed by animals. Yet, grasses evolved only about 40 million years ago, long after the last dinosaur walked the earth. Therefore, no plant-eating dinosaur ever munched on grass.

Figure 43. Right top, one of the best-preserved of the early flowers comes from the Dakota Formation of Kansas and is named Archaeanthus. *The inset box shows the fruiting body thought to go with the flower.*

Figure 44. Right, by the end of the Late Cretaceous, conifers dominated only in temperate and polar regions of the planet. Flowering plants like this Magnolia *dominated the rest of the landscape, and flowers like this were seen by dinosaurs toward the end of their reign.*

Packs of Slashers

Off in the distance of the upland diorama, behind the *T. rex*, is a group of three menacing dinosaurs. Young people almost always excitedly point to the wall and say, "Look at the raptors, Mom!" They are partly correct in their identification. The dinosaurs of the Jurassic Park movies are said to be *Velociraptor*. In life, these little dinosaurs were fierce predators of smaller animals, and they did posses the sickle-claw made famous in the movie. However, the real creatures were not very large, only about six feet from nose to tail tip. While that may be an impressive animal to have chasing you, Speilberg was not happy with these smaller monsters for the stars of his movies, so he "Speilbergized" them: he sized them up for Hollywood. In Speilberg's defense, soon after the release of the first Jurassic Park film, an animal about the size of his *Velociraptor* was found in North America and was named *Utahraptor*. So, large monster-raptors had in fact existed in the Early Cretaceous of North America.

Figure 45. *A* Dromaeosaurus *hunts as part of a pack in this reconstruction at the Sternberg Museum.*

These, and other dinosaurs in the same family, are famous for holding one enlarged claw on the hind foot off the ground (detail), and rotating it forward to slash at their prey.

See the figure on the next page for a modern example of an animal that does something similar.

Regardless of the size question, the animals painted in our reconstruction are not *Velociraptor* for the simple fact that that genus did not live in North America. However, there were several close cousins to *Velociraptor* that did live here, and the ones painted in the diorama are called *Dromaeosaurus*.

All raptors are characterized by having one enlarged, sickle-shaped claw on each hind foot. These claws were held up off the ground by a short tendon that, like a rubber band, held the claw back. However, when the animal wanted to inflict damage to a rival or to catch supper, a muscle in its calf would pull another tendon, rotating the claw into service. You can pretend you are a raptor by curling your toes toward the sole of your foot. Can you feel that it is the muscles in your calf doing the work?

It is not unusual for an animal to lift its claws to protect them. Just think of your house cat at home. Most of the time its feet are soft and furry to the touch, with no evidence of the claws that are hidden inside. But when your cat stretches or works its claws on your couch, they come out with devastating results (fig. 46). Cats have exactly the same mechanism for keeping their claws out of the way until they are needed. This keeps the claws from being dulled on the ground as they walk, and ensures that they are always sharp and ready for use.

The *Dromaeosaurus* are shown hunting in a pack, eyeing the herd of hadrosaurs moving across the floodplain. In contrast, *T. rex* is shown as a solitary hunter, ready to ambush the hadrosaurs that get too close. Museum planners wanted to use this contrast to highlight the different hunting styles. Today, some large mammalian predators hunt together. Animals like lions, wolves, jackals, and hyenas are all examples of animals that hunt in groups. Some large predators, like tigers and bears, prefer to hunt alone.

There are trade-offs to both styles. In a group there are more individuals to help bring down larger prey animals. But, there are also more mouths to feed, a difficulty in lean years. There is not a lot of evidence as to hunting styles in dinosaurs. However, in Alberta, Canada, one site was found to contain at least nine large albertosaurs, a carnivorous dinosaur in the same family as *T. rex*. At another site, four individual *T. rex* specimens were collected together. These, and other sites, have convinced some researchers that at least this large predator may have hunted in packs. It is a truly scary thought to imagine multiple tyrannosaurs coming after you.

George's Second Big Find

The second of George Sternberg's greatest discoveries happened in about 1921 in the Canadian badlands. "The first week in the field found me going over some very promising sandstone exposures when, by the merest chance, I saw three small teeth glistening in the sunlight, two pointing one way and the other meeting them. I did not recognize them at all. They were small but perfectly preserved. I soon had a floor laid bare and in less than an

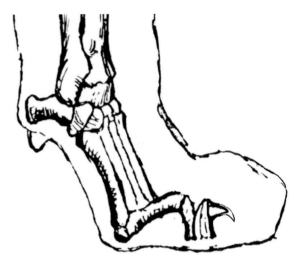

Normal walking

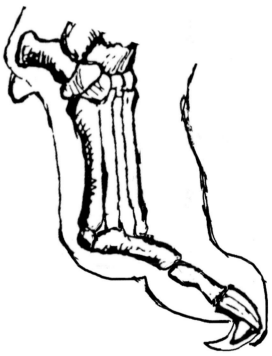

Using claws

Figure 46. *Almost all the modern cats have an interesting mechanism for keeping their claws sharp. When walking, the last bone of the digits containing the claw is held off the ground, and the animal walks on the joint instead of the end of the toe (top).*

When it needs to bring its claws into service, muscles in the forelimb and calf flex and rotate the clawed bones into action (bottom). When finished using the claws, tendons again pull them back out of the way.

hour I knew I had a perfect skull of this little animal as well as most of the skeleton. I had made a very important discovery."

What Sternberg had found was the best-preserved skull of a small and unusual dinosaur named *Stegoceras* (not to be confused with the large, plated dinosaur with tail spikes; that dinosaur is named *Stegosaurus*). Prior to Sternberg's find, people had found small, knobby skull-caps of this strange beast. The skull caps were composed of thick and slightly domed bone, suggesting an animal with a large mound of bone over the top of the head. But now George had found a complete skull (fig. 48).

Figure 47. *George Sternberg poses with the important little dinosaur skull he found in Canada. Note the pictures of the dinosaur mummy (see figure 25) over his desk. Thus, this portrait displays the two greatest finds of his career to that point.*

Sternberg's discovery caused a lot of excitement in the media. He would later write, "We soon learned that the news of this discovery had reached Calgary, Alberta, from the University of Edmonton, and that a representative of the Calgary Herald, MacLean's Magazine, and the Pathe News were the men of the party. We were given a full page write-up in the Herald with pictures showing us at work. And when I left Canada in 1922 for the last time, the short news reel was still being shown in motion picture houses all over the Dominion."

Sternberg's discovery also caused confusion among dinosaur researchers for a time. The first scientist to study the newly-found complete skull mistook the teeth of *Stegoceras* for those of another dinosaur known at that time from only its teeth, called *Troodon*. Thinking that *Stegoceras* and *Troodon* were the same animal, he rejected the name *Stegoceras* in favor of the older, first-used name *Troodon*. Later, George's brother, Charlie, set the record straight. *Troodon* and *Stegoceras* were separate animals. In fact, *Stegoceras* was the first-found representative of an entirely new family of dinosaurs that Charlie named the Pachycephalosauridae.

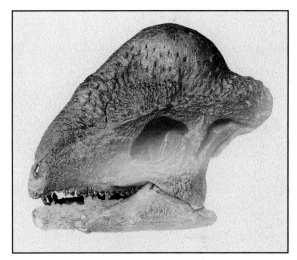

Figure 48. *The* Stegoceras *skull found by George F. Sternberg turned out to be the first representative of a new family of dinosaurs.*

This family name is one of the greatest illustrations of the use of Greek and Latin in all the dinosaur world. That tongue-twisting name can be broken down into its root components: *pachys* meaning thick, *cephalo* meaning head, and *saurus* meaning lizard. Literally, the name means the thick-headed lizard. It has been surmised that the bony mound was used in combat, male against male, for mating rights. Here too, the dinosaur world seems to provide evidence that the sexes were different. There are two groups within *Stegoceras*, individuals with large domes and individuals with small domes. If the heads were used as battering rams or clubs against rival males, the male dome might be expected to be larger, with the females having the reduced bony domes.

George Sternberg would have one more great discovery druing his long career. However, he would have to wait 31 years after his discovery of the best representative of the new Pachycephalosaurid dinosaur family. His third greatest find would be made far from Canada, in the hot summer sun of the Kansas chalk beds.

Figure 49. George Sternberg (?) (left) and a field assistant explore the badlands of Canada, about 1921.

Chapter 7
Along the Kansas Shore

Return to Kansas

During the early part of the twentieth century, the Sternbergs collected many dinosaurs in the badlands of western Canada. A number of their finds were new to science, and in almost every major museum in the world you can find a specimen collected by this energetic family.

As time went on and the contracts to collect in Canada expired, the family business broke up, with the younger boys going their own way. Charles H. retired to California, although retirement would not really describe what he was doing. He continued to collect fossils along the west coast for many more years. Charles M. and Levi stayed in Canada to work for the National Museum of Canada and the Royal Ontario Museum, respectively. George F. went to South America for a time with the Field Museum of Natural History, and upon his return he moved back to Kansas, where he felt fossil collecting was best.

This put George back in the heart of the chalk beds that are so rich in Cretaceous marine fossils. Let us travel back in time once again to that long-gone seaway, and visit the seashore. At the sea's maximum extent, the eastern shore would have been in eastern Kansas or western Missouri. It is hard to know for sure because the rocks from the Cretaceous have been stripped off by weathering. The Rocky Mountains had not yet been built, and the shoreline on the west coast fluctuated between western Utah and eastern Colorado. So, the entire land that later became the Front Range of the Rocky Mountains was still under water at that time.

Life's a Beach

At the beach area of the Sternberg Museum's diorama we see several important interactions between the land and the sea, and the creatures that lived there. Several of the sea creatures, or rather those creatures that made their living from the sea, also needed the land to breed or to rest. For example, overhead are three large flying reptiles similar to what Marsh first found in 1870. These are named *Pteranodon sternbergi*. These are the second largest of the flying reptiles; only one from Texas called *Quetzalcoatlus* grew larger. The flying reptiles hunted at sea, scooping up fish from the water's surface with their up-turned, toothless bills, but they needed to rest and nest on the shore. The large, bulbous crest is what makes *P. sternbergi* distinctive from other large flying reptiles. There is much speculation about what this animal may have done with its crest. Was it for thermal regulation, display for mates, or even some sort of aerodynamic rudder for steering the animal through the air? Perhaps it had no function. But if it did, the most likely explanation is that it was for display, with the males having the larger crests to attract a mate and intimidate rival males. So, from their crests, we can determine that the three flying in a group overhead are all males coming back from a day of fishing.

There are other flying reptiles painted in the mural. Over the water are several whose bills are striped, and they are much smaller than the great pteranodons. The smaller animals are called *Nyctosaurus bonneri*. These were smaller pterosaurs, with wingspans up to twelve feet. By the Late Cretaceous there seems to be only the two kinds of pterosaurs in North America: the large *Pteranodon* and the smaller *Nyctosaurus*.

What's in a Name

Both *Pteranodon sternbergi* and *Nyctosaurus bonneri* have special significance for the Sternberg Museum. In the biological sciences there is a rule that the scientist who describes a species new to science has the right to name the species. Biological species names have two parts, the genus, or generic term, and the species, or specific epithet. For example, the scientific name for humans is *Homo sapiens*. Scientific names are always in a language other than English, usually Greek or Latin, but sometimes words from other languages are used. However, all scientific names must be Latinized. For example, the largest flying reptile known is the giant *Quetzalcoatlus*. Its name is the Latinized form of an Aztec god, Quetzalcoatl.

Another interesting thing about scientific names is that they are not just a bunch of big words scientists make up to confuse everybody else; the names have meaning. The fearsome *Tyrannosaurus rex* comes from the Greek *tyrannos*, meaning tyrant, and the Latin root of *regis* meaning king. *Saurus* is the root for lizard, so the full name translates to the "tyrant lizard king." With just a little knowledge of Greek and Latin, it is possible to guess at the nature of an animal, or where it lives, or whatever, based on the name it was given by the initial authority for that species.

In the case of the two pterosaurs, *Pteranodon sternbergi* and *Nyctosaurus bonneri*, the specific names were given in honor of two men important to the museum. The

Figure 50. Pteranodon sternbergi, *among the largest of the flying reptiles, sail over the beach of the Late Cretaceous Sea in the Sternberg Museum's upland diorama.*

sternbergi name is obviously derived from Sternberg. It was George Sternberg who found the first identifiable remains of this large pterosaur. Having his name used for this species forever honors him, because the naming scientist could have chosen anything at all to call that species. For that reason the *Pteranodon sternbergi* is the animal depicted in the logo for the Sternberg Museum.

Of course, this one honor does nothing to really tell the full contribution made to the science of paleontology by the Sternberg family as a whole. Over the years, the Sternberg name has been used in a scientific name at least 27 times! For them to have been recognized this many times by many independent scientists speaks volumes for the quality and value of their scientific work.

Nyctosaurus bonneri was named for Orville Bonner. The Bonner family worked for many years in the chalk beds of Kansas. They, too, collected many important fossils that are presently in the Sternberg collection and in the collection of the University of Kansas Natural History Museum in Lawrence. Orville Bonner worked at the University of Kansas museum for many years as their preparator of fossils. His recent retirement brought to a close the era of the family fossil collectors.

Figure 51. Ichthyornis, *one of the Late Cretaceous toothed birds, forages along the shore of the Late Cretaceous Sea.*

Our Feathered and Toothed Friends

In addition to the pterosaurs that needed to come on shore to rest, the toothed birds that swam and flew over the inland sea must have nested on shore. Recall that the toothed birds provided Marsh with strong ammunition to battle the scientific doubters of evolution in the 1870s. There are two forms shown in the diorama, a smaller, flying bird called *Ichthyornis* and a larger, flightless bird called *Hesperornis*. *Ichthyornis* was a small, lightly built bird about the size of a modern pigeon. It probably led a gull-like life along the shore of the inland sea, eating small crabs, insects, and fish as it could catch them.

Hesperonris, on the other hand, was highly adapted to life in the water and had lost all ability to fly. Its wings were reduced to nubs, but its feet were well adapted for kicking itself through the water. It lived on a diet of fish or other seafood, and it was probably very awkward when it came ashore. Not being able to stand up, it must have pushed itself along the beach on its belly with its huge back feet. But in the water, *Hespeornis* would have been an agile swimmer, fast enough to catch slippery fish. Both of these species retained the primitive character for birds of having teeth, evidence of their reptilian ancestry.

Figure 52. *This dead nodosaur, a* Niobrarasaurus, *floated out into the Late Cretaceous Sea and ended up in Gove County, Kansas.*

Bloat and Float

Looking along the diorama beach, you will find a dead dinosaur. The museum staff did not place a dead animal on the beach just to be morbid. Rather, the animal painted in the diorama is there to tell a story. This dinosaur belongs to a family called the nodosaurs. This group of dinosaurs resemble overgrown armadillos, because their bodies were covered with bony plates that formed a shell. One day in the Late Cretaceous, this individual died along the shore, and its body was carried out into the sea. It floated on the surface with currents taking it into areas of deeper water; its shell formed a unique funeral barge. After an unknown length of time the bloated carcass sank to the sea floor many miles from where it died. Once at the bottom, like so many other sea creatures before it, it was slowly covered by sediments and entombed along with the fishes and mosasaurs of this strange underwater realm.

Many millions of years later, pieces of the skeleton were exposed in the chalky cliffs of Gove County and almost the entire skeleton of this *Niobrarasaurus* was collected. The Sternberg Museum does not have this fossil, but we did cast its foot to put on display with the other dinosaur remains. There you can see one of Kansas' own rare dinosaurs.

Figure 53. An animal like one of the bird-mimic dinosaurs left this footprint in the sands along the shore of the Late Cretaceous Sea in Colorado.

The Bird-Mimics

In the crazy, mixed up world of the Late Cretaceous, there were birds with teeth looking like dinosaurs, and dinosaurs without teeth looking like birds. This latter dinosaur group is known as the ornithomimids, or bird-mimics. These were medium to large sized dinosaurs and were distant cousins of the toothy, meat-eating *T. rex*. However, the ornithomimids took an unusual twist on the carnivore form. Almost every representative of this group is completely toothless, possessing instead a beak-like set of jaws.

As in so many instances in paleontology, the Sternbergs can boast of finding the best-preserved representative of this dinosaur family. George collected a specimen in Alberta in 1916. His brother Charles named a new species, *Ornithomimus edmontonicus* from that specimen, and this is still the best-known species of that group.

The bird-mimics were mostly in the 10–12 foot range from nose to tail, and stood about 4–6 feet at the hips. The forelimbs were about half the length of the powerful hind limbs. The strength and agility indicated by the skeleton suggests that this group was the fleetest of all dinosaurs, reaching speeds of about 30 miles an hour. Their diet probably consisted of small vertebrates, eggs, insects, and the like. They could open their mouths widely to eat sizable prey, but the muscles of their jaws were relatively weak, and they could not bite down hard.

They had a keen sense of sight provided by large eyes, and their brains were among the largest (in proportion to body size) among the dinosaurs. It is speculated that they were about as intelligent as modern ostriches, which by our standards is not saying much, but they would have belonged to Mensa in the dinosaur world.

Figure 54. Ornithomimus *runs along the beach of the Late Cretacoues Sea looking for food.*

Figure 55. *The Sternbergs (middle left in photo) work to excavate an* Ankylosaurus *in Alberta, Canada in about 1912. Specimens like this were taken to the Red Deer River and floated to railheads for transport to their destinations.*

Chapter 8
Under the Kansas Sea

Fish-Within-a-Fish

In our wild trip through time and space, let us go to 1952 and travel with George F. Sternberg to the chalk beds of Gove County, Kansas. In July of that year, the 69-year old Sternberg was working under the hot summer sun to collect the third highlight specimen of his long career. Earlier that year he had been out exploring with two friends from the American Museum in New York City, Bobb Schaeffer and Walter Sorenson. These men stopped briefly to see George and to hunt with him for fossils in the chalk beds. In the chalk beds Sorenson spotted a section of fish tail coming out of the rock, and called George's attention to it. It was clear that the fish was a *Xiphactinus*, the largest bony fish from the Kansas sea, and the largest bony fish that has ever lived. It was also clear that this specimen was going to take a lot of effort to get out of the rock, and they did not have time that day.

There is an honor code of the fossil hunter that dictates that whoever first spies a fossil has the rights to claim it. Sorenson could have claimed the fossil for the American Museum, but Sorenson and Schaeffer decided that the museum did not have the resources to secure this particular specimen. Besides, they already had a nice *Xiphactinus* on display. George was told to collect it for himself.

So with the green light to proceed, George returned to the site sometime later and worked to uncover the bones, tracing out the vertebrae from the tail to the head. With rock still covering the main part of the body, George could see that it was a complete fish skeleton, and a nice one at that.

No doubt, if Sorenson and Schaeffer had known how complete the fish was, they might have wanted it for themselves. So, George covered the fish to protect it and returned to Hays to call New York. After careful consideration, the New York contingent reasoned that they presently did not have the funds to transport a large

Figure 56. *George Sternberg and helpers work on the Fish-within-a-fish in 1952.*

fossil back to New York, and besides the American Museum already had one *Xiphactinus* on display. No, George, you go ahead and collect it for yourself, he was told.

So Sternberg went back out to finish the job, and as he uncovered the middle part of the fish he discovered how unique this find really was. Inside the ribcage of the 14-foot *Xiphactinus* was another fish, a *Gillicus*, almost wholly intact. This was a fish-within-a-fish! George felt honor-bound to stop work yet again to phone New York. Do you want the fish now, he asked. George pointed out that not only was it a nicely preserved *Xiphactinus*, it preserved the fish's last meal in great detail. But like before, they told George that he had given them plenty of chances to accept the fish, and he should go ahead and collect it for himself.

The summer heat in the Kansas chalk beds is always memorable, and Sternberg no longer worked as fast as he used to. Over the years he had perfected a technique for getting large fossils out of the chalk (figs. 66-68). The entire top of the specimen was cleaned of rock, and rock was also cleared from around the fossil, leaving it elevated on a pedestal. Wooden frames were constructed to go around the fossil, and steel supports were sometimes added on larger specimens. Plaster was then poured into the frame, over and around the fossil. Next came the laborious process of digging underneath the slab of plaster. Great care had to be taken to leave enough thickness on the underside of the specimen so that the fossil was supported and the rock did not fall out of the frame. Then came the moment of greatest risk to the fossil, when the slab of rock and plaster holding the fossil were overturned. Once inverted, the slab was taken back to the lab for final preparation.

Sternberg camped at the site in order to stay close to his prize specimen while he went through these steps during the month of June. By the July 4th weekend, Sternberg was ready to overturn the slabs and transport them back to Hays. He recruited a group of faculty men for the job. Once he had the fossil safely back at the museum, he began the process of final preparation. This involved working from the back side of the slab, removing rock that had been underneath the fish. The final mount shows the side of the fish that was originally down in the rock.

Astute observers of the museum's displays may notice in our recreation of the dig that the fish that George is digging lies on its left side, and the Fish-within-a-fish specimen on display is lying on its right side. This is no accident, but serves to illustrate how the fish was found in the field versus how it is displayed now. The fish's

Figure 57. The Fish-within-a-fish as displayed at the Sternberg Museum.

right side, which was the side first seen by the field party, is now embedded in plaster. We are all fortunate that the collection of the Fish-within-a-fish was captured on film by Dr. L. D. Wooster, and that film was used to make an educational video displayed at the dig recreation in the museum. Visitors can watch the excavation of this famous fossil.

Some people tell me that they have seen other examples of a Fish-within-a-fish, and they ask if the Sternberg Museum specimen was ever cast. It is true they may have seen other specimens, as there are other examples of *Xiphactinus* being preserved with stomach contents. The Smithsonian, Denver Museum of Science and Nature, and the Royal Tyrrell Museum in Alberta all have specimens with stomach contents and look somewhat similar to our Fish-within-a-fish. However, the Sternberg specimen has never been cast or duplicated and is the best example of this type of preservation. The fish on the inside of the Sternberg specimen is less digested than other similar fossils, and the *Xiphactinus* itself is preserved so well as to have been used to answer basic questions about fin placement and structures that had previously not been well understood. The Sternberg specimen is still by far the best, although not the only, fish-within-a-fish.

It should be noted that the specimen has been restored to the way Sternberg originally prepared it. That is, the bones of the fish on the inside are stained a dark brown, and the outline of the missing parts of the inside fish are stained a light brown. Sometime in the past, after Sternberg put the specimen on display, someone painted in the entire fish on the inside with the dark brown stain. This made the inside fish stand out better, but during planning for the current display, museum staff felt that it was misleading as to what was real and what was not. For the fish's new home in the dome, we restored it to the way Sternberg initially displayed it. But there are many people who remember the fish the other way. If you look carefully in the video production shown to the right of the fish you can see the fish both ways. One pan of the camera across the specimen shows it fully stained brown, but later in the video you see Sternberg's crew hoisting it onto the wall with the original dark and light stain from 1952.

While baking in the hot July sun to collect the Fish-within-a-fish, there is little doubt that Sternberg's thoughts turned to the nature of the sea and the fish itself. When paleontologists dig for dry, dusty bones, we try to understand those creatures and their environments. How did they live, how did they interact with other animals of their own and different species? With the Fish-within-a-fish, we have dramatic evidence of two species interacting: one swallowed the other whole. With the other examples of *Xiphactinus* being preserved with large prey in its stomach, and by looking at its mouth full of fish-piercing teeth, we can surmise that *Xiphactinus* routinely ate large prey whole.

What killed this big specimen is a harder question. Did it literally bite off more than it could chew, and in swallowing the 6-foot *Gillicus* suffer some internal damage? Was *Gillicus* somehow toxic to the bigger fish? Because we know that *Xiphactinus* routinely ate large prey species, did its death have nothing to do with its last meal? Or could it be that, because every specimen of *Xiphactinus* found with stomach contents died soon after eating such large prey, it was always fatal and they just never learned good table manners? I am afraid we don't yet know the answer to these basic questions, but these are the questions that drive us to look in the rocks.

Figure 58. *The Sphinx at Monument Rocks, Gove County, Kansas, about 1926. The Sphinx fell over in 1986.*

Common Vertebrae Types
from Western Kansas

Figure 59. Vertebrae are frequently collected from the rocks of western Kansas. How can we distinguish the major vertebrate groups of the Kansas Late Cretaceous Sea based on their backbones?

First, some terminolgy is necessary. The large, cylindrical part of the vertebra is called the centrum *(pl.* centra). *Spiny projections are sometimes present. The spine coming out of the top is the* neural spine, *and the two side projections are called* lateral processes.

Mosasaurs (A in the figure), the sea lizards of the Mesozoic, have centra that range in size from an inch to more than five inches in length. The lateral processes vary in length along the backbone and are often broken off. The most diagnostic feature is that the centrum has one end (front) distinctly cupped and one end (back) ball-shaped.

Plesiosaur (B) centra also vary in length considerably, from just a few inches to almost ten inches. However, the centra of plesiosaurs do not show the distinct cup and ball shape of the mosasaurs. Their centra are almost flat on both ends.

Fishes (C) of all sorts lived in the Kansas sea. Fish vertebrae can be described as "spindle-shaped." That is, they are very deeply cupped on both ends and usually about as long as their diameter. Often, strings of fish vertebrae are preserved linked together. The cavity that is formed when the two ends come together is sometimes filled with the mineral calcite. The result is a calcite formation that looks like two cones attached at their bases (D).

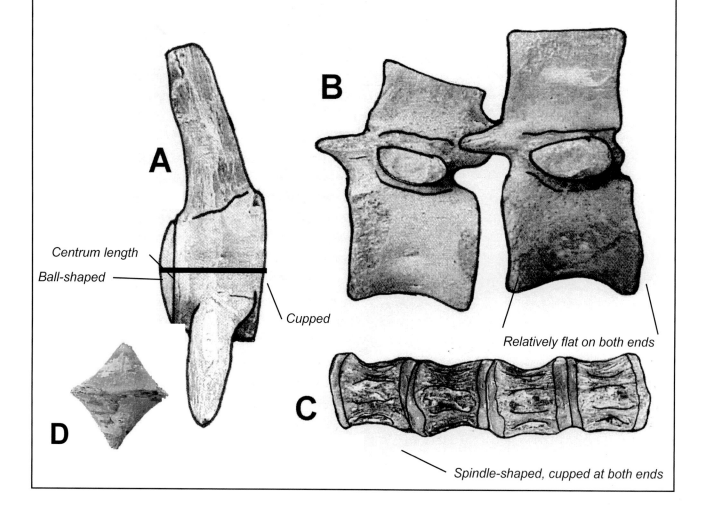

Centrum length

Ball-shaped

Cupped

B

Relatively flat on both ends

A

C

D

Spindle-shaped, cupped at both ends

Into the Deep

In addition to North America, many other parts of the world experienced sea encroachment and many areas experienced the deposition of the sediments that form chalk. The name for the Cretaceous Period derives from the Latin *creta*, meaning chalk. For example, the famed White Cliffs of Dover are formed of material similar to the Kansas chalk, and they are about the same age. Many of the fossil fishes found in Kansas were first described in England.

To understand the environment that these fishes lived in, we would like to look at a modern analog. However, a good modern analog for the Late Cretaceous Sea that covered the central continental areas of North America does not exist. Today, there is only one place in the world where marine water covers continental crust, but it is hardly a good analogy for the situation in Kansas. The one modern place is Hudson Bay, and the chilly waters of the north stand in stark contrast to the tropical waters of Kansas' past. Nothing about the chemistry of the water nor the kind of life that lives in these shallow waters is similar between the two localities, so we must make educated guesses about the conditions in the Kansas sea.

The depth of the sea has been the subject of some debate. Everyone agrees that it was a shallow sea, but "shallow" in sea terms might mean anywhere from 20 to 1000 feet deep. These depths are shallow when compared to the open ocean that can be measured in miles in some of the deep ocean trenches. A good general guess about the maximum sea depth in Kansas would be from 500 to 1000 feet.

We know a good deal about the floor of Kansas' Late Cretaceous Sea. It was there that the action took place as far as fossil hunters are concerned. For an animal to become a fossil in the Niobrara Formation, its body must have fallen to the sea floor and been undisturbed by scavenging organisms long enough to become buried in the soft mud. Did the burial take place very quickly, or was the bottom of the sea inhospitable to scavenging animals?

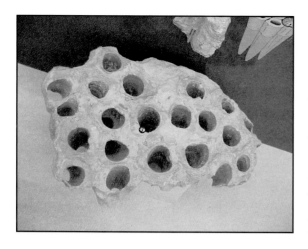

Figure 60. *The clam* Durania *sometimes formed colonies that grow together forming a honeycomb-like structure on the sea floor. This firm foundation provided a solid support for other life forms during the Late Cretaceous.*

Life on the Sea Floor

We know that during the deposition of the Smoky Hill Chalk Member of the Niobrara Formation, the bottom was home to many clams. They were many in number of individuals, but the species diversity was low. The clams tended to take on one of three different forms. Either the clam grew very flat and disc-shaped, or it grew very deep and bowl-shaped, or it was an oyster growing on top of one of the other two. The clams were likely adapting to their environment. Our challenge is to understand what environment caused these reactions.

The most widely accepted suggestion is that the bottom of the sea was "mucky," with an indistinct bottom. If you could go back in time and somehow walk along this bottom, you would find yourself sinking into the mud. If you were a clam, you might take on a snowshoe-like habit and grow large enough to spread your weight over a larger surface area. Or you might try the iceberg approach and allow yourself to sink into the mud, but leave just enough above the surface to allow you to feed. And this is precisely what we think the first two types of clams were doing.

Figure 61. *Dr. L . D. Wooster (left), president of Fort Hays Kansas State College (now FHSU) from 1941 to 1949, poses with George Sternberg beside a large clam shell from Kansas. This shell is displayed at the Sternberg Museum and illustrates the "snowshoe" adaptation for life on a mushy sea floor.*

Several species of clams adopted the iceberg approach, but one group was particularly interesting. The rudists had a unique take on the clam form. Instead of having two almost-equal shells, one or both of the shells became cone-like. The other shell either became cone-like, giving the entire animal a double-horn look, or the second shell was reduced in size and formed a cap over the cone of the bottom shell. Sometimes when these clams lived together the bottom, cup-shaped shells, grew together forming a honeycomb-like pattern (fig. 60).

In some rudists, the cap shell was so reduced that it formed a translucent screen. Why would a clam need a "sky light?" It is possible that the clam was not alone in living on the sea floor. The sky light may have served to provide light for brown algae, called zooxanthellae, living within the tissues of the clam. Many modern corals host these algae within their tissues in a symbiotic relationship. The algae photosynthesised their food and needed access to sunlight, while they gained safety

Common Shark Teeth of Western Kansas

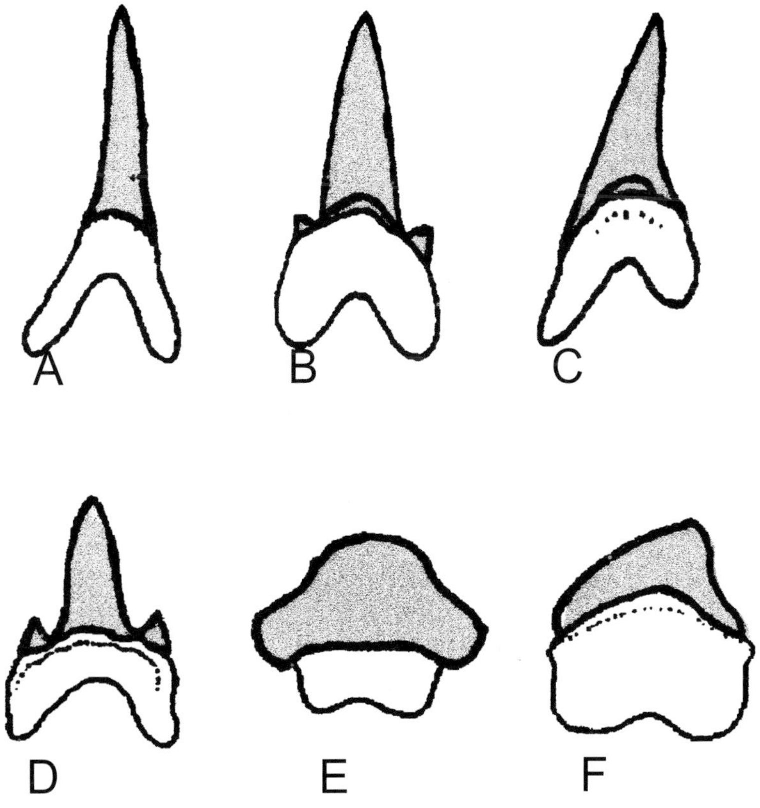

Figure 62. Shark teeth found in Kansas vary widely in their shape. The most common are illustrated to the left. Anyone trying to identify shark teeth should understand that there is a great deal of variability, even among teeth from the mouth of one individual shark.

This illustration is not to scale. Different kinds of sharks have different sized teeth, anywhere from just a fraction of an inch to more than 3 inches. Often, the shape of the root is as important in shark tooth identification as the shape of the crown. Numbers in parentheses are approximate tip-of-crown to base-of-root measurements in inches.

A. Scapanorhynchus (1)

B. Cretolamna (1½)

C. Cretoxyrhina (1–3)

D. Cretodus (¾–1)

E. Ptychodus (½–1)

F. Squalicorax (¼–¾)

within the tissues of the clams. In return, the algae stimulated the host's metabolism, especially the rate of shell production. To date, there are no upper shells of rudists identified from the Kansas chalk, although there are many examples of the lower shell. Perhaps, the Kansas rudists also had highly modified upper shells and they have not been found because the upper shells were almost non-existent.

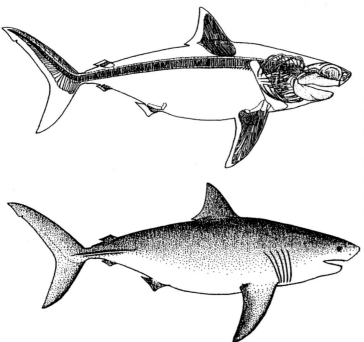

Figure 63. Sternberg Museum houses the best example of the Late Cretaceous shark, Cretoxyrhina. *Here, its skeleton is restored (top) and its probable body outline is recreated based on research on the Sternberg specimen.*

The third type of clam, the oysters that grew on top of the other clams, had an easier time. They just had to seek out one of the first two clam types that formed a solid substrate to land on and anchor themselves for life.

A number of small fish skeletons have been found on the inside of large clam shells, sometimes more than 100 individuals within one pair of clamshells! The question is obvious: How did all those fish get caught together and die? It may be that the fish were living with the clam, swimming in and out of its shell, perhaps eating parasites off the clam and gaining shelter in the shell in return. Such arrangements are not uncommon in the tropical waters today. But exactly how the fish all came to die together is a mystery. However, it does suggest that there were other animals living on the sea floor, and one might imagine a "mini reef-like" community developing, with the larger clams acting as the hard substrate and the basis of the community.

The diversity of life at the bottom of the Kansas sea pales in comparison to modern tropical reefs, though. The Kansas seafloor was just not as hospitable to life. Perhaps it was because of the water depth. If the seaway was generally 600 feet or more deep, then the bottom would have been below the zone to which sunlight can penetrate, so the bottom may have been permanently dark and lacking the life-providing rays from above. Or, perhaps, it was the muddiness of the bottom. Most modern tropical reefs need very clear water unpolluted by sediment. Whatever the reason, the Kansas sea did not seem to have the diversity of living forms that the modern oceans have.

Figure 64. A mount of the small but toothy Enchodus *on display. This fish had huge fangs and must have been a formibable predator on small fish.*

Figure 65. A set of teeth from the fossil Ptychodus *clearly shows why they are called "pavement teeth." The teeth link together to pave the roof and floor of the mouth, allowing the shark to crush shells and feed on the soft-bodied inhabitants.*

Shark!

Several kinds of sharks lived in Kansas' Late Cretaceous Sea. I recall how ironic I thought it was the first time I went shark tooth collecting in Kansas, about as far away from any ocean as you can get today!

One group of sharks is called the "shell crushers," and for good reason. These sharks did not have teeth just around the rim of their mouths, but had the entire inside of their mouths paved with teeth, top and bottom, like a cobblestone street (fig. 65). This gives their teeth the common name of "pavement teeth." The shark's scientific name is *Ptychodus*. Its teeth are rounded and massive, not at all sharp, but designed to take a heavy load. It is likely that these six-foot sharks were shell-crunching specialists, feeding on

oysters that lived on the clams in the whole of the bottom of the sea.

Other species of Kansas fossil sharks look more like the stereotype, with a mouthful of slashing teeth. One species of shark, called *Cretoxyrhina,* grew to the size of a modern-day great white shark (fig. 63). They looked and probably also behaved very much the same. Like its modern relatives, *Cretoxyrhina* was one of the most perfect predators. It was a 20 foot long eating machine, built for speed and armed with its mouthful of teeth, some almost three inches long. We know from stomach contents that it ate many kinds of fishes, other sharks and, when it could, small mosasaurs.

There were several sharks in the 8-12 foot range that probably patrolled the waters looking for easy prey or even carcasses of large animals upon which to feast. There is evidence to suggest that *Squalicorax* scavenged on large carcasses. There are several examples of *Squalicorax* teeth having been found in association with

Figure 66. Sternberg had prefected a technique for getting large specimens out of the chalk. First, the rock was carefully cleaned off the top of the specimen.

Wood forms were added to hold wet plaster poured over the specimen to form a slab. Large fossils were divided into two or more sections.

(Continued on next page.)

Figure 67. Next came the laborious process of digging underneath the fossil's slab, until it could be freed.

Figure 68. The slab containing the plaster-covered fossil was brought to the lab for the final step, removing the rock from the underside of the slab and exposing the fossil's unweathered side.

Figure 69. The work was very labor-intensive, and George Sternberg was famous for his ability to sleep anywhere.

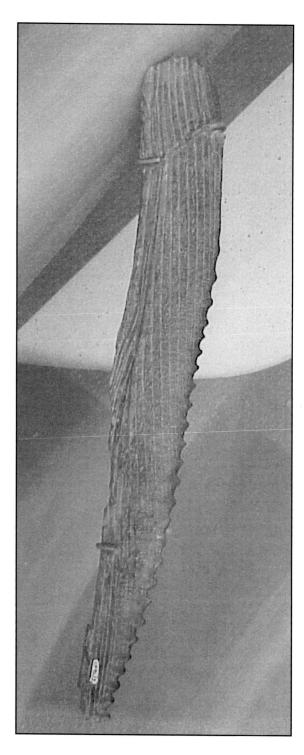

Figure 70. *The use of the serrated fins of* Protosphyreana *is still a mystery. Some researchers have suggested that they were used to stun prey or perhaps to forage through the mud at the sea bottom .*

jaws of the larger shark, *Cretoxyrhina*. It is reasonable to think that the larger shark was dead when it was being bitten by the smaller species. We also find evidence of *Squalicorax* bite marks on mosasaur bones. Wheter they were biting the mosasaurs while the lizards were alive is hard to say, but it seems likely that the sharks were feeding on already-dead prey.

Sharks have a formidable dentition. There are literally hundreds of teeth in a single shark jaw. They grow in from behind the active cutting teeth in a conveyor belt-like manner, rolling forward to replace teeth lost when biting a victim. It is no wonder, then, given the countless number of sharks that lived in the Kansas seaway, all of them shedding hundreds of teeth throughout their lives, that shark teeth are one of the most common fossils in western Kansas.

Fishing for Answers

There was a fair amount of diversity in body size and shape among the fishes of the Kansas sea. *Kansius* was small, just a few inches long, and its skeletal fossils are found only inside clam shells, whereas *Xiphactinus* is the largest bony fish that ever lived, reaching lengths of 16 to 18 feet. Despite the large numbers of fossil fish that have been collected from the chalk, surprisingly little is known about their biology, how they may have lived, and how they interacted. This is simply because there are few scientists who have devoted their careers to studying these animals. If you are an aspiring paleontologist, the Kansas fishes are badly in need of study.

Swimming in a small school in the underwater diorama, and displayed as a fossil in the fishes case, is *Enchodus*. It was a smallish fish, only 12 to 18 inches or so in length. It possessed a mouthful of long, needle-like teeth. It must have been a tough light-weight however, because two teeth in the roof of the mouth and two in the jaw formed formidable fangs for capturing smaller fish. In fact, the teeth of the lower jaw were so long that when the mouth was closed, the teeth projected through the snout and were exposed above the nose of the fish. *Enchodus* ate smaller fish, and was in turn prey for larger fish.

Another fish, *Saurodon*, is thought to have been about five to six feet long, although its body past its head is unknown to science. It had some unusual characters in its skull, including a lower jaw that protruded beyond the upper teeth. Its teeth were relatively small, blade-like, and smooth. How it used its teeth and protruding lower jaw is a mystery. It has been suggested that it fed near the surface and the lower jaw helped it to get around prey in a stealthy manner, but what that prey may be is unknown.

We also know very little about the body of the fish *Protosphyraena*. All that is known is the skull and its front fins. In contrast to *Saurodon,* with its elongated lower jaw, *Protosphyraena* had a long, spear-like snout projecting over its lower jaws. It also possessed a pair of forward-projecting front teeth in the upper jaws near the base of the snout. In addition, this fish had long, stout front fins that were serrated along the front edge. What possible use they made of those fins and snout is unknown. Perhaps they swam into schools of fish, stunning them with their large fins. Or perhaps they used their snout and fins to forage in the soft bottom mud for small worms and other tasty morsels.

Another enigmatic fish is *Ichthyodectes*. In many ways it looks like its cousin, *Xiphactinus*, but *Ichthyodectes* lacks the large, slender, fish-holding teeth of the former. *Ichthyodectes* teeth are small points compared to the elongate teeth of *Xiphactinus*, which would indicate that *Ichthyodectes* ate something other than large fish, perhaps soft-bodied squid or planktonic organisms of some sort. This discussion of the Cretaceous fish from Kansas illustrates how little is really understood about this interesting group of prehistoric creatures.

Figure 71. *Above, the skull of* Protosphyreana *shows why it is called the "snout fish."*

Figure 72. *Below,* Ichthyodectes *looks very much like its close cousin,* Xiphactinus *(the big fish of the Fish-with-a-fish).*

Lizards of the Deep

The kings of the Cretaceous seas were the mosasaurs. Mosasaurs were latecomers to the Age of Dinosaurs and the Kansas sea. No mosasaur fossils have been found in Kansas below the Fairport Chalk Member of the Carlile Shale, about 90 million years old (fig. 9), and by far the most specimens are from the Smoky Hill Chalk. As a group, mosasaurs invaded the marine waters of the Late

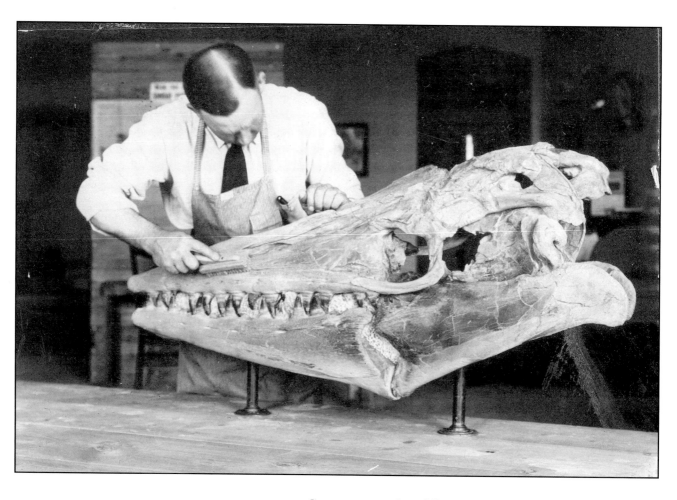

Figure 73. George Sternberg puts the finishing touches on a large mosasaur, a Tylosaurus, *for exhibit in "his" museum in Hays.*

Cretaceous and rapidly diversified into many wonderous forms. Their heyday was relatively short-lived, however, as they succumbed to the mass extinction at the end of the Cretaceous, 65 million years ago.

Mosasaurs were lizards, thought to have been closely related to today's monitor lizards. This means that mosasaurs are related to the common fence lizards that scamper about the prairie today, but mosasaurs were lizards on megadoses of steroids. Some species grew to 45 feet in length. Their limbs were modified into paddles for underwater maneuvering; their tails grew thick and muscular to propel them through the water. They were exclusively aquatic. Their skeletal structure shows that they would not have been able to hold up their weight on land, so like the whales and dolphins that came after them, mosasaurs appear to have lived, mated, given birth, and died at sea.

Several kinds of mosasaurs lived in the sea. Some kinds were smaller, in the 10–15 foot range, whereas one kind was giant, the 30–45 foot *Tylosaurus*. Visitors can view the *Tylosaurus* skeleton from figures 73 and 75 in the fossil gallery and as a recreation in the undersea diorama. Mosasaurs had a unique way of eating large prey. We humans tend to think of the skull as a bony ball that contains the brains, because that is how our heads are constructed. We have very limited mobility in our heads, and the jaw is the only moveable part.

Most other animals are constructed differently. In mosasaurs, the head is a very loosely connected group of bones, many of which could be moved independently (fig. 74). The lower jaw was attached to the remainder of the skull by a question mark-shaped bone that allowed the mosasaur to rock its lower jaw forward and backward. Thus, the lower jaw could be thrust out, ahead of the upper jaws. The lower jaw also had a joint in the middle, about halfway between the chin and the back of the jaw. This joint allowed the jaw to bow downward. In addition, the lower jaw was loosely connected at the chin so that the left and right jawbones could separate in the middle.

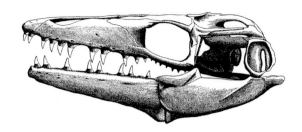

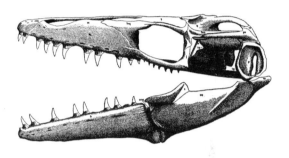

Figure 74. The upper figure shows a restoration of the mosasaur Platecarpus with its mouth almost closed.

The lower figure shows the same individual with its mouth gaping, the joint in the middle of the lower jaw flexed, and the entire lower jaw rotated forward.

Figure 75. Three large slabs containing the mosasaur skeleton in figure 73 sit in the lab waiting to be mounted on display. These same slabs are still on permanent display in the Sternberg Museum.

And there was even more to the range of movement in the mosasaur head. The upper tooth-bearing bones could be moved forward and backward independent of each other. There were also teeth in the roof of the mouth that could be moved forward and backward at will. Thus the entire system worked to expand the head around food and tractor it down the gullet. The mosasaur would lunge forward after a large fish, rocking its lower jaw forward, and clamping on with its upper teeth. It then rocked its lower jaw backward and forward in a cutting-like motion while alternately moving the left side upper teeth forward, and then the right, until the entire prey animal was swallowed. We know from fossilized stomach contents that mosasaurs ate basically anything they wanted, from fish and sharks to hard-shelled coiled ammonites, to other mosasaurs. And once in a while a mosasaur fell prey to one of the very large sharks, so it was truly a world of eat-or-be-eaten, even among the top predators in the sea.

Some species of mosasaurs seem to have specialized in deep-diving behavior. We see the evidence in their bones. When animals, including humans, are subjected to high pressures like those in deep water, they can experience a condition known as "the bends." The high pressure forces nitrogen out of the blood stream and into the tissues of the body. If a diver surfaces too fast, the nitrogen cannot work its way back into the blood stream and is retained in the tissue. After repeated dives, nitrogen can build up in the tissue, blocking its access to oxygen-rich blood and effectively killing the area around the blockage. Human divers must be careful to time their dives to avoid this painful condition.

Some mosasaurs, particularly *Tylosaurus* and *Clidastes*, suffered the bends regularly. In the bones of those animals, areas of oxygen depletion are evident in pockets of dead bony tissues of the vertebrae. Whatever pain they suffered does not seem to have hindered their lifestyle. They must have lived with the bends for many years before finally dying. However, some kinds of mosasaurs, like *Platecarpus*, do not show evidence of the bends in their bones. The *Tylosaurus* shown in the diorama at the Sternberg Museum is depicted in deep water, close to the sea floor.

It is a basic rule of ecology (the science of how organisms interact with their environment) that similar species living in the same area can maximize success if they go after slightly different food sources in the environment. The fact that we find evidence of the bends in some species more frequently than others suggests that mosasaurs were doing just that, partitioning the resources between species, with some species specialized in feeding near the bottom of the seaway while others hunted different prey closer to the surface.

Rubber-Necking

The other group of large swimming reptiles that inhabited the Kansas sea was the plesiosaurs. Unlike the mosasaurs, plesiosaurs are not closely related to anything alive today. They have been described as looking like a snake strung through the body of a turtle. There are two general forms of plesiosaur, the long-necked and the short-necked. Their snake-like necks were attached to relatively broad, flat bodies. As a group, plesiosaurs extend back in time to the Triassic and their diversity peaked during the Jurassic. Through the Cretaceous the numbers of plesiosaur species declined gradually until the end of the period. The decline in plesiosaur dominance may be partly explainable by increased competition with the mosasaurs in the Late Cretaceous.

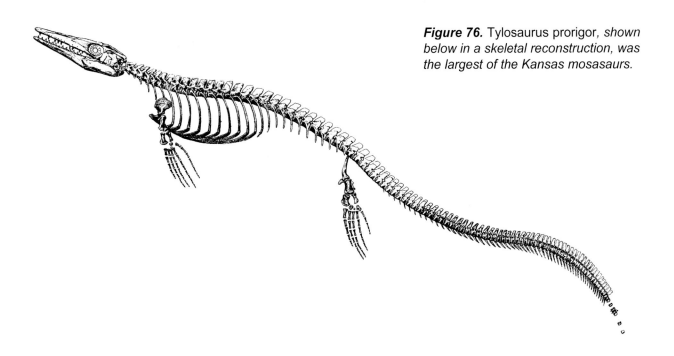

Figure 76. Tylosaurus prorigor, *shown below in a skeletal reconstruction, was the largest of the Kansas mosasaurs.*

Figure 77. *The Kansas sea was home to both long- and short-necked plesiosaurs. The short-necked type, like the* Dolichorhynchops *shown here and on the beach in the upland diorama, had short, stumpy necks and tails. However, some of them grew to 20–30 feet in body length.*

The long-necked form was the longest animal to ever have lived in the Kansas Late Cretaceous Sea. Some reached 50 feet in length. Much of their total length consisted of their long necks. They may have hunted fish by swimming along slowly using their long necks to ambush schools of fish from afar.

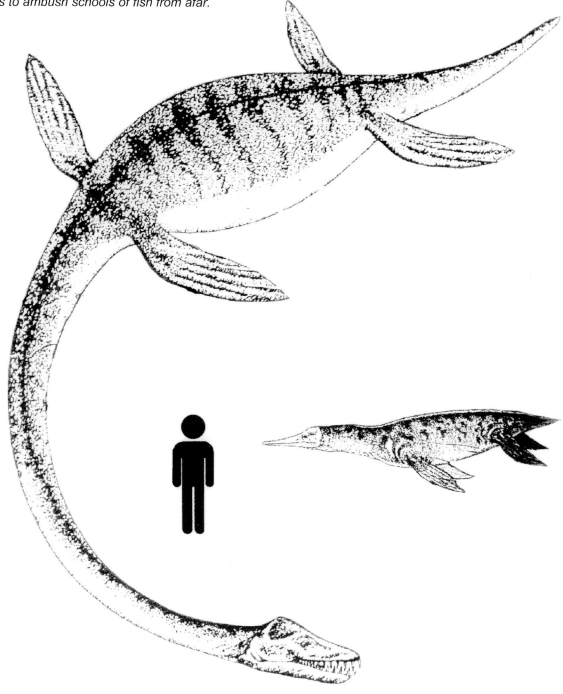

The needle-like teeth of plesiosaurs suggest that all were fish-eaters, and some, such as *Dolichorhynchops* (seen in the museum's exhibit gallery as a fully mounted skeleton (fig. 79) and as a model on the diorama beach), also have a long, slender muzzle particularly adapted to catching fish.

Just the reverse of the mosasaurs that propelled themselves through the water with a powerful thrashing tail, plesiosaurs had short stumpy tails but very strong limbs developed into powerful paddles. The hip and chest bones of plesiosaurs were well developed, providing a sturdy base for the great masses of muscle used to power the paddles. In contrast, mosasaurs had almost no bone in the hip and chest regions, so their paddles were relatively weak, probably used only for steering the animal.

We placed our recreation of a short-necked plesiosaur named *Dolichorhynchops* on the beach in the diorama. Although we do not know if plesiosaurs ever came on land, say to lay eggs or to sunbathe, it seems reasonable that with their large bony chest and hips, they could have supported their own weight out of the water. On the other hand, one specimen from Kansas suggests that, in at least one species, plesiosaurs gave live birth at sea. That specimen awaits a full study.

Short-necked plesiosaurs ranged in size from the small *Dolichorhynchops* at about 10 feet long to the large *Brachauchenius*. Although a complete skeleton of *Brachauchenius* is still unknown, estimates of its size are in the 20-30 foot range.

A full mount skeleton of *Dolichorhynchops* and the skull of *Brachauchenius,* both short-necked plesiosaurs, can be seen in the Cretaceous fossil gallery. This *Dolichorhynchops* specimen was found by M. C. and O. W. Bonner, friends of George Sternberg, who donated the specimen to the museum

Figure 78. *Above, from left to right, George Sternberg, Orville Bonner, "Windle," and Marion Bonner pose around the work table where the* Dolichorhynchops *skeleton is being mounted.*

Figure 79. *Below, the short-necked plesiosaur* Dolichorhynchops *grew to about 10 feet in length. The Sternberg Museum's specimen is the best preserved example of this plesiosaur in the world.*

in 1955. Prior to their discovery only two other, less complete, specimens were known, and both of them were found by Sternberg. In the long-necked plesiosaurs, the neck alone could reach 20 feet in length. The total body length could be as much as 30–50 foot. It is hard to imagine an animal swimming very fast with a 20 foot long neck stretched out in front of it, so most interpretations suggest that the long-necked forms were ambush hunters. Either they lay on the bottom in near-shore settings and waited for fish to swim within reach, or they swam along slowly until they encountered a school of fish, then used their long, snaky necks to strike their prey.

Another interesting thing about plesiosaurs is that with their skeletons are occasionally found rounded stones, often in piles or groups. These stones are probably gastroliths, or stomach stones. Every group of modern vertebrates (fish, amphibians, reptiles, turtles, birds, and mammals) have species that are known to eat stones from time to time. However, there is much debate about what purpose the stones serve. Suggestions for their use range from aiding in digestion, being used for ballast in aquatic animals, relief from hunger, accidentally being swallowed with food, or being picked up because they are attractive to the animal.

Several groups of prehistoric animals have been found with gastroliths, including plesiosaurs and some dinosaurs. The stones found with plesiosaurs are interesting because they were carried many miles from where the animal first picked them up to where the animal finally died. Often the nearest place for the plesiosaur to have acquired the stones is several states away, indicating that the animal traveled great distances during its lifetime.

Uprooted Flowers

An interesting fossil that is found only rarely in the chalk beds is the colonial crinoid *Uintacrinus*, named for the Uinta Mountains in Utah, where they were first found. In Kansas, they occur in large, thin slabs of limestone, sometimes with hundreds of individuals on one bedding plane. Crinoids sometimes are called sea lilies because of their superficial resemblance to plants, but they actually are animals related to starfish and brittle stars. Crinoids have a head, called a calyx, that contains the mouth parts. Long "arms," or tentacles, stretch from the calyx and reach out into the water currents for microscopic food particles. The arms catch foodstuff and transport it toward the mouth. At the other end of some kinds of crinoids is a stalk, or holdfast, often formed of rings linked together. The stalk anchors the animal to some hard surface on the sea floor to live out its life, and the combination of the stalk, head, and tentacles makes the animal look superficially like a plant.

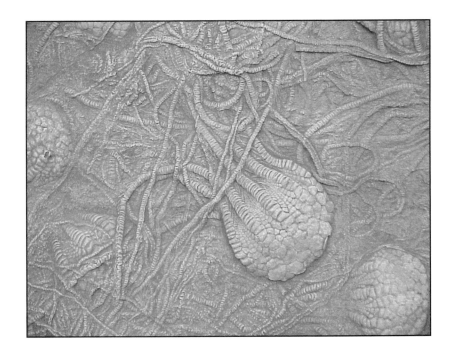

Figure 80. Uintacrinus *was an unstalked crinoid. The calyx formed a round body, and long tentacles were used to gather food particles and transport them to the mouth in the center of the calyx.*

Uintacrinus was a kind of crinoid that lacked an anchoring stalk. In fact, there are numerous modern crinoid species that lack stalks. Many of the modern species use some of their tentacles to grasp the substrate while directing other tentacles into the current to catch particles of food in the water. They also can use the tentacles to move across the sea floor like otherworldly spiders, or thrash their tentacles to swim through the water for short distances.

So why do we find *Uintacrinus* in large death assemblages? They must have lived and died together, but what killed the colony? Early ideas were that *Uintacrinus* lived as a colony of individuals floating along with the current, their tentacles intertwined. If the

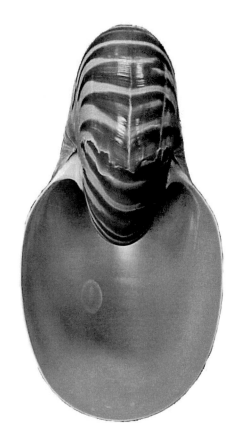

colony were to encounter an area where the water was poisoned, they would have died *en masse* and settled to the sea floor, subsequently becoming fossilized. Such poisoned water could possibly occur, for example, during something known as a "red tide." Some groups of floating algae occasionally undergo population explosions in marine waters. The algae produce a water-soluble toxin that is ten times as effective as cyanide. During population explosions, the toxin can build up in the water, killing fish and other organisms that are nearby. A modern red tide in 1947 off the Florida coast killed an estimated 500 million fish.

Some recent work has suggested that *Uintacrinus* did not live as a floating colony. For one thing, the skeletal weight of the *Uintacrinus* made it unlikely that it would have been buoyant enough to float without considerable expenditure of energy to stay aloft in the water column. So, perhaps *Uintacrinus* was already on the seafloor, and living in a intertwined colony as a means of staying on top of the mucky, muddy bottom, much like the clams discussed earlier. If they were already on the seafloor, it might have been simply an increase in sedimentation rate that caused the whole colony to be covered and preserved, like during a storm.

Whatever the cause of their death, the slab displayed at the Sternberg Museum is perhaps the best example of *Uintacrinus* in the world. The animal has been found in Cretaceous rocks of Utah, Kansas, and the chalk beds of England. The Kansas specimens tend to be the best preserved. The original color of the rock was light gray. The red color of the Sternberg specimen comes from a stain applied so that the individual animals can be seen better.

Other Invertebrates of the Kansas Sea

In addition to the clams mentioned earlier, several other significant invertebrate groups are found in the Kansas chalk. Both the ammonites and the squids are cephalopod mollusks, related to today's squids and octopuses.

The ammonites are represented in the fossil record of western Kansas, but mostly as impressions of the shell in the rock (fig. 84). The chemistry of the depositional environment was not ideal for preservation of the shell itself. Ammonites are coiled, shelled animals. The shell grows in whorls and is segmented into chambers. The animal lives in the last chamber, but a part of its body extends through the entire shell, anchoring the animal in place. Another part of the ammonite which is occasionally found is called the aptychus (plural aptychi) (fig. 83). The paired aptychi are thought to have been coverings, or lids, for the ammonites, but some have suggested that they were more like the "jaws" of the ammonite. Both shells and aptychi are on display in the rocks case near the tent.

The "head" of the ammonite had tentacled arms which it used to capture food, mostly fish. Because they are rarely found in the chalk little is known about their importance in the ecosystem of the Late Cretaceous Sea. There is one modern animal similar to the ammonites called the chambered nautilus (the name given to Captain Nemo's ship, you may recall). The nautilus (fig. 81) lives mostly in the western Pacific Ocean and average about seven inches in diameter. They are active swimmers, sucking water into their bodies and forcing it back out a special opening underneath the "head," so that they move backwards (maybe we move backwards to an nautilus?) by jet propulsion. They also move through a wide range of water depths, from 20–1,800 feet deep, feeding with their 90 suckerless tentacles.

Figure 81. *Opposite is a side view (top), a cross-section view (middle), and a front-end view (bottom) of the shell of a modern nautilus. In the cross-section, notice that the shell is formed of chambers with a connecting opening between each chamber.*

In life, the animal could pump water through the chambers to make itself more or less buoyant to either float upward or sink. The main body of the animal was in the last chamber of the shell seen in the front-end view.

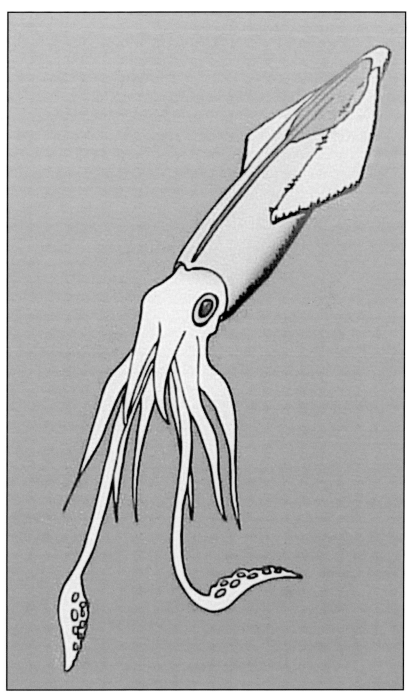

Figure 82. A squid has an internal skeleton consisting of a spoon-shaped end and a long, stiff rod. Squids have 10 tentacles.

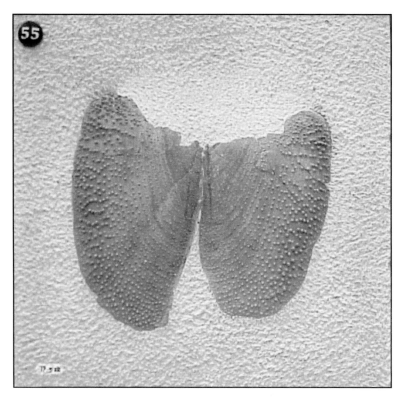

Figure 83. The type specimen of Spinaptychus sternbergi *is displayed at the Sternberg Museum. Aptychi are thought to be shell coverings of ammonites.*

Figure 84. Often ammonites are preserved as casts in the chalk. Actual body fossils of these invertebrates are rare in western Kansas chalk.

Mosasaurs are known to have fed on ammonites as shells have been found with bite marks. It is as if the mosasaur repeatedly bit down on the shell, crushing it with each bite, until the soft animal inside lost its grip on the protection of the shell. The soft animal was sucked down the mosasaur's throat and the shell was discarded like the husk of a sunflower seed to sink to the bottom.

Another interesting invertebrate group is the squids. Unlike ammonites, squids have an internal shell surrounded by soft tissue. But what they lacked in body armor they make up for with agression. Squids are close relatives of octopuses, and these two groups are some of the most predaceous animals of the sea. Octopuses are named for their eight arms or tentacles, whereas squids have ten arms. Two of the squid's arms are modified into highly effective grasping organs. Normally the squid might carry these two arms coiled close to the body, but when it needs to, the arms can spring out and capture prey with special hooks on the enlarged ends of the arms (fig. 82).

Modern squids and octopuses are the most intelligent of the non-segmented invertebrates. Octopuses kept in aquaria have been observed to learn and even to play with objects in their tanks, seeming to enjoy the mental exercise of having fun. This group also contains the largest of the modern invertebrates. Tales of mariners speak of seeing large sea monsters. These monsters are almost without a doubt sightings of the giant squids (sometimes called karken) or giant octopuses (called devilfish). A modern karken can reach lenghts of 72 feet and a devilfish may have a tentacle span of 80 feet. No wonder tales were told of these fantastic beasts!

Like the ammonite shell, the internal skeletons of squids do not preserve well in the chalk, but occasionally they are found. One, *Niobrarateuthis bonneri* (fig. 85), would have been a sizable animal, with a body perhaps three feet long. If it were like a modern squid, it would have had tentacles perhaps 10 feet long. It is possible that the deep-diving mosasaurs were at least in part squid-eating specialists. Modern sperm whales are known to feed on giant karken in deep ocean waters. What unbelievable battles must take place in those deep, dark, modern waters as the whale attempts to subdue this worthy prey.

Proof is in the Numbers

The number of fossils that have come out of the Kansas chalk is truly staggering. One scientist tried to get a rough idea of how many specimens have been collected from the chalk for study and preservation in museums since serious collecting began in the 1870s. He could not go through all museums everywhere to get an estimate, so he went through several large collections and extrapolated numbers to estimate the totals. His estimates suggest that about 4,222 fishes, 1,823 mosasaurs, 878 pterosaurs, 225 Mesozoic birds, 210 turtles, and 58 plesiosaurs have been collected and placed in museum collections to be available for study. If his numbers are anywhere near correct, it is easy to see that there is a well preserved fossil record of the Late Cretaceous marine fauna.

One might ask, "Do we need to collect more fossils if such riches already exist in museums?" The answer is "yes," for several reasons. Many of the fossils that were collected in the past were not located very exactly within the rock section. This may have been because the rocks themselves were not yet fully studied and broken into formations (see fig. 9), or because the modern political boundaries were not yet established to give a good geographic reference for the find. Sometimes the locality data with a specimen only shows that it was collected in Kansas, but more precise information about the ranges of the animals is needed to fully understand their history and evolution. In addition, large collections of fossils are needed for certain kinds of studies, such as studies looking at the range of variation within a species, or variation of a species over time. Every individual specimen becomes important in these sorts of studies. Many of the early specimens were collected as trophies as much as scientific specimens. In an effort to get the fossil out of the ground and mounted as a nice display, important data were irretrievably lost for all time. Today, almost as much attention is paid to the rock around the fossil as to the fossil itself, so new collecting is called for. Finally, there are many species that

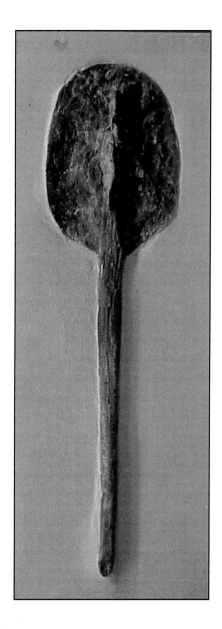

Figure 85. Squids have internal shells consisting of a spoon-shaped end and a rod that helps to stiffen the body. This specimen is the type of Niobrarateuthis bonneri. See figure 82 to understand how the shell was positioned in the squid's body.

Figure 86. (Next page) George shows his father around the new museum facility in McCartney Hall on the Hays campus, about 1930. When the museum moved to the dome in 1999, the museum space in that building was renovated into classrooms.

are still incompletely known from the fossil record. Every new discovery that finds its way into a museum has the potential to add to our understanding of the past and to the enrich us all.

If the Cretaceous Sea was so exciting and the fossil record prolific, why do we not see more about these animals than we do dinosaurs? Why is it that Spielberg did not make "Cretaceous Sea Hunt" instead of "Jurassic Park?" Well, I cannot speak for Spielberg, but the reason seems simple. Far more researchers work on dinosaurs than on the Kansas marine fossils. Dinosaurs have always been popular favorites and have enjoyed a great deal of media "ink." But, as you can see, the sea life of Kansas was every bit as exciting. The questions are out there. Can you help find any answers?

Color Plate Captions

Plate 1. *The Smoky Hill Chalk Member of the Niobrara Formation is world-famous for its fossil content. The chalk hills are beautiful colors of yellow, tan, and orange, mixed with blue-gray shale in pastures of rust and brown grasses. Western Kansas is a place of striking splendor.*

Plate 2. *The toothed diving bird* Hesperornis, *found in western Kansas, was used by Othniel C. Marsh to close the evolutionary gap between modern birds and their reptilian ancestors. In the Sternberg mural, the birds are shown displaying sexual dimorphism. That is, the males and females display different color characteristics. Birds commonly have differently colored plumage in the sexes, and it is likely that many prehistoric birds did as well.*

Plate 3. *When on the campus of Fort Hays State University, the museum had two popular dioramas. One showed the grassland landscape of Africa, with a young lion walking away from an anxious group of zebras and antelope.*

Plate 4. *The other diorama was a recreation of the prairie north of Hays, along the Saline River, in 1865. The painter of both murals, Bill Eastman, was a graduate of FHSU, and took careful pains to paint his subjects accurately. Neither diorama could be saved in the move to the museum's new home in the dome. However, large sections of each mural were saved to be used in future exhibits at the new building.*

Plate 5. *The Sternberg Museum now features a very popular Discovery Room. This place is for individuals and families to explore the natural world on their own. Museum staff make specimens and resources available to visitors, and they can delve into a topic as deeply as they wish. The room is designed to help visitors develop their natural curiosity and sense of wonder about the world around them.*

Plate 6. *The giant mosasaur* Tylosaurus *is known to have feasted on smaller mosasaurs from time to time. Here the monster is preparing to eat the smaller mosasaur, a* Platecarpus. *Large tylosaurs were about 45 feet in length, whereas* Platecarpus *did not grow nearly as large. This and other differences suggest that different mosasaur species were making their livings in different ways in the Cretaceous Sea.*

Plate 7. *The large short-necked plesiosaur,* Brachauchenius, *grabs at a squid, a* Niobrarateuthis. *The head of* Brachauchenius *was about 4½ feet long, with an estimated body length of 25 feet or more. Fossils of both these animals have been found in western Kansas and are on display at the Sternberg Museum.*

Plate 8. *George Sternberg poses with some of his finds from the season of 1928. Behind him and on his lap are mosasaur heads. The four large heads at the corners of the photograph belong to a family of extinct mammals, brontotheres, that lived in North America from 53–34 million years ago. Behind Sternberg, a turtle can also be seen.*

Plate 1

Plate 2

Plate 3

Plate 4

Plate 5

Plate 6

Plate 7

Plate 8

Plate 1

Plate 2

Plate 3

Plate 4

Plate 5

Plate 6

Plate 7

Plate 8

Chapter 9
A Growing Museum

Elam Bartholomew and the Fungus Among Us

We now depart from our story of fossil collecting and the earth's past, and turn our attention to another individual who played a part in the history of the Sternberg Museum. Elam Bartholomew (fig. 88) was born in Pennsylvania in 1852, and like so many others of the day, moved many times with his family, always further west. In 1874, just a few years after Marsh's first fossil collecting trip into western Kansas, Elam moved with his young wife to Stockton, Kansas, about 40 miles north of Hays.

Like the other pioneers who moved west, most of his life was devoted to making a living by growing crops on the arid plains, raising a family, and involving himself in the religious and community life of the area. But Elam was a man of many interests, and relatively late in life he nourished an interest in the plants and fungi that grew in the vicinity of his Stockton farm. He become particularly intrigued with fungi and spent many evenings reading texts on mycology by candlelight.

In 1898, at the age of 46, he applied for graduate studies at Kansas State Agricultural College and completed his degree later that year with a thesis on "The Plant Rusts of Kansas." Just a few years after that, in 1901, Elam became editor and publisher of an unusual journal entitled *Ellis and Everhart's Fungi Columbiani*. Two New Jersey botanists originally started this endeavor, but as their health failed, Elam accepted the opportunity to carry on their program. He eventually shortened the title to *Fungi Columbiani*, and continued publishing the series until March, 1917.

This was not really a magazine or journal so much as a means of disseminating fungi collections to specialists in mycology. Each issue of *Fungi Columbiani* included 100 specimens of fungi, each sealed in its own envelope with a detailed label giving identification, collector, locality, and date. There were 70 subscribers to this service. Roughly twice a year, Elam, working closely with his wife, and sometimes his children, would hand-make paper envelopes, label them, package each fungus specimen separately, and then bundle 100 packages to make each copy. This was repeated for each of the 70 subscribers. Because each edition had 100 specimens, it was called a century. On average, he sent out almost 14,000 fungi specimens each year.

In 1911, Elam began a publication of his own creation. It was managed like the first, and was entitled *North American Uredinales*. It was dedicated to one group of fungi that Elam was particularly interested in: the rusts. He continued this publication through January of 1926. Elam spent most of his botany career collecting, trading, and shipping rust fungi around the world and corresponding with other mycologists.

In all, with steadfast help from his wife Rachel, Elam sent out 36 mailings of *Fungi Columbiani* (Centuries 16-51) and 35 mailings of *North American Uredinales* (Centuries 1-35). Between the two publications he mailed out 427,700 specimens, all in hand-made, labeled packets.

During his career as a mycologist—begun at an age when most people retire—Elam made many collecting trips around the United States and into Canada and Mexico. He traveled an estimated 133,000 miles in his journeys and personally collected an estimated 292,000 fungi specimens. On one trip in 1908, Elam recorded this in his diary: "Botanized all day to the east of town [Rogers, Arkansas] down as far as the Electric Springs being most successful in my labors as I secured over 1,100 specimens of fungi for distribution in *Fungi Columbiani*. This is the largest number of specimens ever collected by me in one day!"

In 1927, the same year that George F. Sternberg settled in his new home in Hays, Elam was awarded an honorary doctorate degree from the Kansas State Agricultural College for his significant achievements and contributions to the science of mycology.

Two years later, Elam followed Sternberg's example and moved to Hays to take up a position overseeing a campus herbarium. Elam donated much of his library and botanical collection to the college in Hays, and he settled down to an academic life at the age of 77. Elam died a few years later, in 1934, so his time in Hays was

Figure 87. The 1930 field trip of the Kansas Academy of Science annual meeting took participants to the chalk beds of western Kansas.

Elam Bartholomew (lower left) went along. Behind Bartholomew is a Mr. Collyer, and a Mr. Streeter is in the foreground. No one else is identified in the photograph.

relatively short. However, the herbarium that he started is an important part of the Sternberg Museum, and it is known formally as the Elam Bartholomew Herbarium.

The Coalescence of the Sternberg Museum

As far back as 1907, the administration of what is now Fort Hays State University supported the idea of a campus museum. In the school catalogue for the 1907-1908 school year, one room in the basement of the first campus building, Picken Hall, was labeled as the "museum room." This room was shared between the small collection of the museum and the small campus library. However, very soon the growing library overflowed into the museum.

The first museum collections consisted of curios, rocks, mounted birds, and stuffed skins. A local real estate dealer, C. W. Miller, had purchased a number of mounted specimens and had worked to learn for himself the trade of taxidermy. He placed his mounts in local businesses around town and gave specimens to offices and departments of the new college. Those specimens eventually found their way into the museum room. In the spring of 1914, C. W. Miller was named curator of the museum, but he had been functioning in that role for some time, at least since 1910.

Figure 88. Portrait of Elam Bartholomew.

Also in 1914, Ward Sullivan, a professor at the college, began to amass a collection of historical items. Mr. Sullivan feared that the pioneer way of life was vanishing, and he wished to preserve as much of the past as possible. He recruited other faculty members of the college to donate items of interest to the museum. Even the college president, William A. Lewis, took an active interest in the development of the museum.

Sternberg Years

In the summer of 1926, George Sternberg had just returned to the United States from collecting in South America for the Field Museum of Natural History. He set up a small shop in Oakley, Kansas. George was a showman and loved to have people admire the fossils that he collected and prepared. He began to invite school groups out to his dig sites and helped the young people find shark teeth and other fossils. George even shared specimens with local schools, including a large *Xiphactinus* that was displayed in the Oakley school for many years. Dr. L. D. Wooster, a professor from the Hays college, took a class of geology students to visit George in the field, and this proved to be a pivotal moment for both George and the campus museum.

Figure 89. *Myrl Walker in the field in an undated photograph.*

Upon his return, Dr. Wooster lobbied President Lewis to invite the famous fossil hunter to Hays to build up the budding museum on campus. This also offered George something he had never had—a position at an institution of higher learning. George had gotten his education through decades of hard work in the fields, but he lacked formal schooling. George's father, Charles H., had a good formal education, but Charles pulled George out of school often to accompany him on fossil collecting trips. Katherine Rogers, who knew George and authored his biography, wrote "Just how long George stayed in school is unknown. He was always a little vague when asked about it in later life. Maybe fifth grade, maybe a little more…"

So, the offer to have him come to Hays gave George the chance to have a professional affiliation at an institution and a place to showcase his fossil collecting and preparation talents. George could not be named as a faculty member on campus because he lacked a college degree. However, he was given the title of Curator of Geology and Paleontology. In 1932 he was awarded an honorary Master of Science degree by Fort Hays State University.

Figure 90. Portrait of Myrl V. Walker.

C. W. Miller, who had been the first curator of the museum, died in 1933, and in the same year C. E. Rarick became president of the college. Rarick appointed George as the Director of Museums, to oversee all the collections on campus. At that time the collections included the geology and paleontology collection, the modern taxidermy mounts of Miller, and the history collection of Sullivan. Dr. Fred W. Albertson oversaw the herbarium collection that Bartholomew assembled.

Myrl Walker

Several other people enter the story of the museum at this point. When L. D. Wooster visited Sternberg in Oakley, a young senior student named Myrl Walker was along on the trip. Walker was excited about the prospect of having Sternberg come to Hays, and it started an association between them that lasted the rest of their lives. Walker spent a lot of time with Sternberg in the field and lab, learning the skills of fossil collection and preparation. Together, they traveled to many western states during the summers and collected for both the American Museum and the Smithsonian. Walker took time off to pursue graduate studies at the University of Kansas, and he then returned to Hays to teach. In 1933, Walker obtained a position with the National Park Service and worked for many years for that organization.

Figure 91. Bill Eastman poses with some of the models of modern wildlife he sculpted for the museum.

In 1955, Myrl Walker was enticed back to Hays from his stint with the Park Service, and Walker was given the title Director of the Museums. Sternberg's title became Curator of the Museum of Geology and Paleontology. In the summer of 1961, much against his wishes, Sternberg was forced into retirement by the state employment guidelines. Walker took on Sternberg's old duties.

Bill Eastman

In the summer of 1943, Sternberg was working alone in the dusty cliffs near Douglas, Wyoming, when a steer on a rampage headed down the draw in his direction. Sternberg scrambled up the cliff face and clung to a skimpy sagebrush, hoping that he was high enough to avoid the steer's horns. Soon a rancher, looking for the lost steer, came by and maneuvered his horse between Sternberg and agitated beast. Dropping from his precarious hold, Sternberg slid down the cliff, dusted himself off and introduced himself to the rancher. The horseman's name was Bill Eastman, and he invited Sternberg to supper. Soon, Eastman and Sternberg discovered they had similar interests, with Eastman being trained in art and interested in museum management. Eventually, Sternberg invited Eastman to move to Hays to continue his graduate studies in art and to work for the museum producing paintings of the wildlife of the plains.

Figure 92. Above, Eastman's most famous works for the museum are undoubtedly the paintings for the North American and African grassland dioramas.

He hid "signatures" in the paintings instead of signing them the conventional way. In the African exhibit, he branded one of the zebras with the brand of his own ranch (700).

Figure 93. Below, for the North American exhibit, he faithfully painted the landscape from north of Hays along the Saline River, but he hid a kangaroo among the bison herd.

After World War II, Eastman, his wife, and their daughter arrived in Hays. Eastman produced many works of art for the museum and later traveled to Africa and Australia to study the wildlife on those distant continents. The best known works by Eastman at the old museum on campus were the murals done as backdrops for African and North American grassland dioramas.

Museum and university officials studied the murals, hoping they could be moved from the old museum into the dome, but the murals were constructed in such a way as to make this impossible. When the murals were dismantled, several large sections were preserved, including Eastman's famous signature marks. Instead of signing his name to the paintings, Eastman painted hidden

Figure 94. The library of the early campus in Picken Hall. Note the museum specimen sharing space with the books.

"signatures" into the murals. In the African mural, one of the zebras was branded with the brand from Eastman's ranch and, in the American grassland mural, he painted a kangaroo among the bison. Many school children over the years were challenged to find these hidden elements.

The Museum Gets a Name

George Sternberg stayed active for a few years after his retirement. One of the last entries in his field book is dated May 13, 1963, and relates to the fish *Saurodon*. Shortly thereafter he suffered a stroke that left him incapacitated, and he finished his life in a nursing home. He died on October 23, 1969.

In her biography of her father-in-law, Clifton Witt, Grace P. Witt of Hays wrote, "During Morton C. Cunningham's presidency, he wanted to rid the museum of 'all Sternberg's old bones' so the building [McCartney Hall] could be converted into administrative offices. This plan created so much opposition that he had to back off." It seems that the faculty appreciated Sternberg's personal contribution to the community and the contribution of the museum to campus life. In an interesting side note, Witt states that her father-in-law was the one who built George Sternberg's house on Elm Street.

Myrl Walker was the faculty advisor to the Sternberg Geology Club, a campus student group. The club had proposed that the campus museum be renamed to honor the Sternberg family, but apparently the proposal did not meet with much success with the college administration.

Witt wrote, "At about the same time, Leonard Thompson [from the Department of Business and a good friend of Sternberg] was trying to get the museum named for the Sternbergs. The president [Cunningham] kept refusing, and Leonard kept trying. One day when I stopped by the Witt house, Leonard was there, fighting mad. He had just come from the president's office. He told me, 'That man actually told me to get

Figure 95. George Sternberg's living room in his house on Elm Street.

Figure 96. The reading room of Forsyth Library was located on the second floor of what is now McCartney Hall.

Figure 97. Museum in the first floor of the library building (now McCartney Hall), about 1928.

out and stay out, or he would have me bodily removed!'"

Cunningham retired on June 30, 1969. Witt wrote, "As soon as John W. Gustad took over the presidency, I went to see Sam Sackett, then the Faculty Senate representative for the English Department, whom I knew valued George Sternberg's contributions to the school and to the town.

"I asked, 'Sam, can't the Faculty Senate make proposals for naming college buildings?' When he affirmed that it could, I continued, 'Don't you think our museum should be named for the Sternbergs?'

"He pounced on it. 'What a great idea! I'll propose it next meeting.'"

In his history of the university, James Forsythe wrote "Soon after George F. Sternberg died in October, 1969, at Hays, Kansas, a proposal made by the Sternberg Geology Club to recognize the family was given serious consideration. Late in the fall of 1969, President John W. Gustad, with the approval of the Board of Regents, endorsed the proposal of the Sternberg Geology Club and the museum became officially known as the Sternberg Memorial Museum."

So in the end, the campus museum was renamed. And there were more changes in store for the budding museum, both in name and ultimately in location.

Now it Gets Confusing

Meanwhile, in the department of biology at FHSU, various faculty members began building collections of arthropods, fishes, amphibians and reptiles, birds, and mammals. These collections, with the already-extant herbarium, formed the core of what came to be known as the Museum of the High Plains. The curator of the Bartholomew Herbarium was Dr. Howard C. Reynolds from 1957 until 1982. The Museum of the High Plains had no public exhibits, but used its collections in teaching and especially research. Drs. Charles Ely and Eugene Fleharty were instrumental in the early growth of the collections. Subsequently Drs. Tom Wenke, Jerry Choate, Frank Potter, Gary Hulett, and Joe Thomasson all added to the collections. The Museum of the High Plains was formally recognized as a division of the university in 1973, and Dr. Jerry R. Choate was named as director.

Walker retired in 1973 from the Sternberg Memorial Museum and was replaced by Dr. Richard Zakrzewski, who became the Director of the Sternberg Memorial Museum and Professor in the Geosciences Department. Under Zakrzewski's guidance, the museum focused on updating its curatorial records and standards. Zakrzewski's research focuses on Tertiary fossils—animals that existed long after the Cretaceous Sea disappeared, when Kansas had become a terrestrial environment—and he continues to expand the museum's reputation for research on fossil vertebrates. Moreover, he hired the museum's first exhibits preparator and its first secretary.

In 1980, university administration merged both campus museums into one budgetary unit, with Jerry Choate as Director of Museums and Director of the Museum of the High Plains and Richard Zakrzewski as Director of the Sternberg Memorial Museum. This was done to enable the museum to apply for federal grants, and Choate moved quickly to improve the likelihood of obtaining grants by hiring an educator, developing educational programs, and establishing a series of temporary exhibitions to complement the permanent exhibits of the museum.

There was one more major change in the museum administration. In 1994, with the move to the dome imminent, the university formally merged all the separate museums on campus under the umbrella of the Sternberg

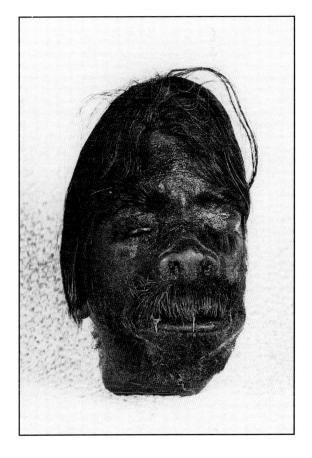

Figure 98. One of the most popular exhibits in the old museum was the shrunken head from South America.

Museum of Natural History. This name reflects the emphasis of all the campus museums since at least the 1960s, the natural environments of the present and past on the Great Plains, while retaining the Sternberg family name. It should be noted that this merger was accompanied by a de-emphasizing of the museum's efforts in history, archeology, and ethnology to facilitate greater emphasis on natural history. The objective is to transform the Sternberg Museum into one of the top natural history museums in the nation.

Divisions of the Museum

Most of this book has focused on the early days of fossil collecting, the fossils of Kansas, their impact on evolutionary thought, and how that story has been implemented in the first phase exhibits at the Sternberg Museum. However, as you can see from the preceding history, the Sternberg is not just a fossil museum. It is a museum of natural history in which all major groups of plants and animals are collected and studied. Presently, the museum has curators (the scientists who are in charge of particular collections) in modern and fossil plants (Dr. Joe Thomasson), insects (Dr. Richard Packauskas), fishes (Dr. William Stark and Mark Eberle), reptiles,

Figure 99. Charles H. Sternberg gets a visit from his grandchildren, children of George Sternberg.

turtles, and amphibians (Travis Taggart, Joseph Collins, and Dr. Eugene Fleharty), birds (Dr. Greg Farley), mammals (Dr. Jerry Choate, Dr. Donald Kaufman, and Dr. Glennis Kaufman), and vertebrate fossils (Dr. Richard Zakrzewski and Mike Everhart). The museum also houses collections of rocks and minerals, invertebrate fossils, and modern fresh-water clams.

The Sternberg Museum is involved in many areas of study in all the collection areas. For example, when the Kansas Department of Wildlife and Parks samples fish populations in the river systems of the state, they send representative fish to the museum for identification and safe housing for future study. The museum has one of the most extensively used collections of Great Plains mammals in the United States, and the mammal collection also grows yearly. The museum's work on fossils also is continuing, with new specimens being collected all the time. The collection of insects is growing rapidly, and the collections of birds and amphibians and reptiles are important reference collections containing voucher specimens (specimens that have been mentioned in research papers). The Sternberg probably houses the largest collection of fossil seeds ever assembled from the Great Plains. Additionally, the museum enters into partnerships with both governmental and private organizations to house materials collected from their lands.

Figure 100. George visits his parents at their home in San Diego.

Figure 101. Sternberg was not without a sense of humor. He created this composite skeleton from the bones of several different kinds of animals.

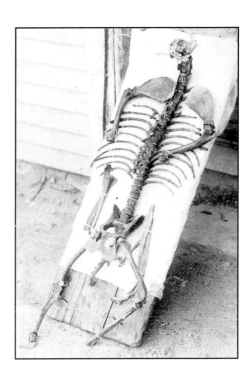

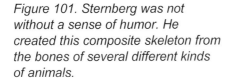

Figure 102. *"Happy Jack," an old cowman who lived in a log cabin near the Red Deer River in Alberta, Canada, and operated "Happy Jack's Ferry," a well established landmark in that remote region. Photograph taken about 1913.*

Chapter 10
Role of a Museum

Most of the research and work discussed in the previous chapter goes on out of the public eye, so it is important that the museum go to special lengths to help the public understand the role and significance of its work. After all, it is the public who provides the majority of support for institutions such as Sternberg. It is easiest to break the functions of a research museum into four steps. Like an iceberg, the part that is above the surface for the public to see is just the tip of what exists below.

First, museums collect. Staff, students, and associates collect fossils, mammals, plants, insects, or whatever, and bring those things back to the museum for the second step. Also, donations to the mueum's collection are accepted if the specimen helps to further the museum's mission of research.

Museums preserve. There is a lot implied by that two-word sentence. Preservation means to save all pertinent data with the specimen, to keep track of where it is in the collection, and to ensure that the collection is safe from all manner of hazards. Each collection has its own needs. For example, birds and mammals are stored as dried skins and are subject to infestations of insect pests. Insects never bother fossils, but changes in temperature and atmospheric conditions can hasten the chemical breakdown of the minerals that preserve the fossils. Curators of some fossil collections (Sternberg's is not one of these, thankfully) must even worry about radioactive minerals that have penetrated the bones and made the collection itself hazardous! Any collection can be irretrievably lost in the case of fire or flooding.

Because each collection is different, each collection has its own specialists assigned to monitor its condition, handle loans and new acquisitions, keep track of the data, etc. This is more than a full-time job. Some museums are fortunate enough to have a conservator, a museum professional whose specialty is not in biology but in chemistry and physics. The conservator watches out for chemical and physical degradation of collections. He or she views the specimens not as biologic or geologic entities, but rather as little packages of chemistry that the environment is trying to destroy. The Sternberg Museum hopes to retain a conservator in the future.

The third step in the process is research: generating new knowledge. Most university museums use their facilities to train graduate and undergraduate students in the museum profession or to enable research required for degree programs. The curators and professors also conduct research in their fields of expertise, and researchers at other institutions make use of the collection through loans of specimens and on-site visits to the collections. However it takes place, research is the core of the next, and final, stage of the museum's service to society.

Museums teach. This is the tip of the iceberg that the public sees when they come to the museum, and they usually see only a part of that. Public exhibitions are what most people think of when considering how they get information from the museum. Exhibits are an important way to communicate the interesting facts learned through basic research conducted by the scientists. Exhibits strive to take complex ideas and distill them into easy-to-understand graphics and text supported by real specimens, and allow the public to browse and learn in an enjoyable atmosphere.

But teaching takes place in other ways as well. One way is when researchers publish their findings in scientific journals or present their work at meetings. Here the teaching is among scientists. Museums also offer a variety of educational programming, such as talks, demonstrations, newsletters, books, videos, etc. In addition, museum staff frequently answers questions from the general public and from governmental bodies. These questions range from identifying a particular fossil, to how do we get rid of bats in our attic, to what type of animal is eating my garden. Museums exist so that the public can benefit from the museums' holdings through the dissemination of information.

Museums serve as a major database of society. Natural science museums store data about the natural world and use the data to learn more about the world around us. How else, for example, can we know if the environment is changing, or realize that a species is becoming rarer, or understand the life of the past, without having the data that museums house? If you hear that a researcher has determined that the environment is changing, she must have had access to information about what the environment was like in the past, and that she got from a museum. This is why we, as a culture, value museums, and why public and private support for museums must continue. For the service to society, for the new knowledge generated about our world, for the sheer fun of learning it on a Saturday afternoon's visit, museums matter!

Building the Dome on the Range

We have almost come full circle, through millions of years of geologic history up to the date given on the first page of our story: March 13, 1999, the grand reopening of the Sternberg Museum in the dome. But there is still one story left to tell: the building of the new museum in

Figure 103. Many thousands of people enjoyed the museum when it was on campus. Visitors were often surprised at the quality of the collections in such a small and unassuming museum.

the dome. During 1983–1984, an unusual building was constructed on the northeast side of Hays. It was really two buildings put together. One was a dome, four and a half stories tall, with two floors, the second floor being open to the ceiling arching high overheard. The second building was a three-story structure with one section being a single large room, open through the second story.

Figure 104. The rectangular portion of the facility originally housed this large swimming pool and hot tubs. The dome housed a variety of other recreational attractions. This space is now the beautiful lobby of the museum.

The dome was built as an athletic club and boasted two tennis courts, four racquetball courts, weight training and aerobic dance areas on the second floor, and a twenty-four-lane bowling alley, a bowl and pro shop, and locker rooms on the first floor of the dome. The other building housed a large swimming pool and hot tubs, a restaurant, beauty salon, the club's business offices, and a radio station.

However, the endeavor fell on hard economic times and went bankrupt in 1987. The building sat vacant and neglected, except by vandals, for several years. In 1990 the current president of Fort Hays State University, Dr. Edward H. Hammond, saw potential in the dome. Here was a chance to move the museum to a prime position for attracting visitors, literally a stone's throw away from the busy interstate. The hard work of acquiring the building began.

The Chrysler Corporation, in a bank merger, purchased the mortgage to the building. For several years, the mortgage had not been paid and property taxes were owed to the county, so Chrysler was eager to dispose of the building. The county accepted the building in lieu of back-taxes and sold it at a public auction. The FHSU Endowment Association was on hand to purchase the building, bidding $1 plus processing costs. So for a little less than $10, the museum had a new home.

However, the building was in bad shape. The roof leaked, the pool had not been drained, pipes were broken, and mold and mildew permeated the structure. Vandals had broken in and did what vandals do. The entire building needed to be gutted for the new museum. Some work was done right away by university crews to stabilize the building, but the next step was a long process of planning for the new facility, and the planning began as soon as the building was acquired.

Figure 105. The second floor of the dome was open to the ceiling, arching 3 ½ stories above. Two tennis courts, 4 racquetball courts, dance studios, and weight training equipment were organized under the dome.

Every detail needed to be worked out. From the needs of the collection storage areas to the mechanical equipment rooms; from considering the experience of the visitor in the exhibit galleries, to where to store mops and brooms: Every square foot of the building was gone over by different professionals, each working from his or her own perspective. Museum staff and university personnel worked together to develop the best museum plan possible.

Of course, nothing happens without money. Dr. Hammond worked hard to acquire the funds to push the museum project forward. In the end, whereas the building only cost about $10, the total museum project was to be

Model *T. rex* Facts

Height: 18 feet to top of head

Length: 42 feet nose to tail

Weight: about 5,000 pounds

Covering: most is durable fiberglass, but the head and neck regions are silicon to allow movement

How long to build: about one man-year

valued at over $11 million. Thus, the museum is a monument to the efforts of the entire university and the community of Hays. It is a natural continuation of the interest the people of Hays have shown in the museum since the early 1900s.

The opening of the new museum building in 1999 marked the start of a new chapter in our history. On that snowy day in March, we opened to the world a wonderful new facility with our first phase permanent exhibits, including the Cretaceous fossil gallery, the undersea diorama, the upland diorama, and the wildly popular Discovery Room. To date, hundreds of thousands of people have tromped through the galleries and enjoyed their experiences under the glare of *T. rex*.

The Future of the Sternberg Museum

Planning is presently underway to continue the permanent exhibits around the perimeter of the dome's circle, and there is a big story yet to tell. The Cretaceous gallery highlights the fossils from that exciting time when the sea covered the state, but there are many fossils from other time periods in western Kansas as well. During the late Miocene (about 5–14 million years ago), Kansas was a savanna, not unlike the grassland plains of east Africa today. Many animals roamed Kansas that one would now expect to find in Africa, such as elephants, camels, bone-crushing carnivores, zebras, and

Figure 106. Museum staff and consultants held many meetings and discussions about what the new museum building should be like, and what visitors to the exhibits should experience.

rhinoceroses. The museum houses fossils from Kansas of all these, and their stories deserve to be told.

Then there was the Pleistocene Ice Age, a time when glaciers scoured the North American continent. The life of Kansas was different yet again. Giant ground sloths,

giant bears, mastodons and mammoths, and sabertooth cats all called Kansas home.

And of course, there are the modern ecosystems of the plains. The Great Plains is a vast grassland habitat, full of beauty and wonder all its own. We want to tell the story of the interactions of the plains species; the balance between the black-footed ferret and the prairie dog, between the yucca moth and the yucca plant, and among deer and their natural predators. Future permanent exhibits will also examine the causes and consequences of our changing environment and actions we can take as a people to preserve the way of life on the plains for all organisms, including humans.

But of course, all of this planning takes time and a variety of resources. If you have been inspired by the Sternberg story, if the history of life from then until now gives you pause to wonder about the world around you,

Figure 107. *The large dinosaur models were custom-made by Deaton Museum Services of Minneapolis, Minnesota.*

First, scale models of the animals were built and reviewed by museum scientists. Then the scale models were used to build life-size models.

A base of steel and styrofoam was made to give the general body outlines. Clay was added over the entire surface, and the details of the skin were sculpted by hand in the clay.

Once the clay model was finished, the entire thing was covered with latex and fiberglass. The latex picked up the fine detail of the sculpted model and the fiberglass ensured that the latex would hold the original shape. Together the latex and fiberglass formed a negative cast, or mold.

The negative cast was pulled off, destroying the sculpture in the process. Then fiberglass was poured into the mold, hardening into perfect casts of the original clay model. Finally, the body casts were pieced together, recreating the model in durable fiberglass.

you might consider ways of supporting the museum and its mission.

You can contact the museum for information about becoming a member of our friends organization, or consider donating your time through the volunteer program. Many of our volunteers do not live in Hays, but still find ways to contribute their talents to the museum.

You might consider helping fund the museum through a planned charitable gift from your estate.

However you wish to become involved, contact the museum at (785) 628-4286 or write to the Sternberg Museum of Natural History, 3000 Sternberg Drive, Hays, Kansas 67601. You can visit us on the web at www.fhsu.edu/sternberg.

The museum is here for you and all people.

Figure 108. Moving-in day for the dinosaurs was an exciting time for museum staff and the entire community.

The body parts of the dinosaurs were shipped to Hays from Minnesota and then had to be lifted into the second floor through the "dino door."

From there they were lifted inside the building to the newly constructed third floor. After the big animals were in place the walls for the dioramas were constructed around them.

Figure 109. *Museum staff of all ages put in many long days and nights to see the museum through to completion.*

Figure 110. *There are some perks for working in a museum!*

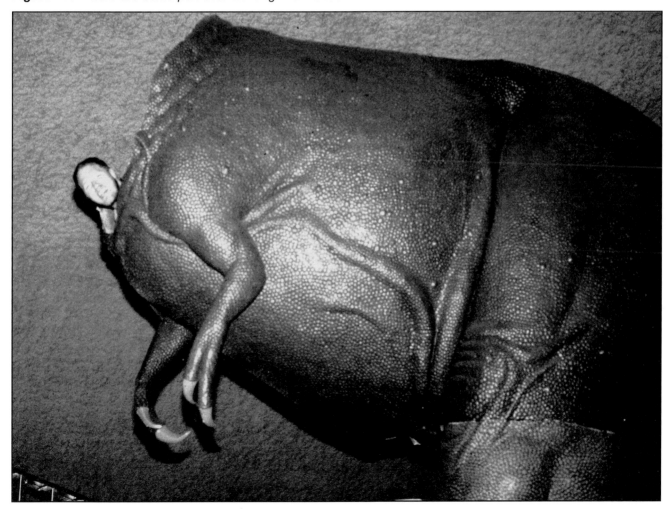

Appendix

Pronunciation Guide

Some of the words in the text are tongue-twisters. If you would like to keep up with your 5-year old and be able to pronounce the names of some of the prehistoric animals and geologic terms, this guide is for you.

Albertosaurus (al-ber-tuh-saw-rus)

Allosaurus (al-o-saw-rus)

Archaeopteryx (ar-kee-op-ter-iks)

Brachauchenius (brach-au-keen-e-us)

Brachiosaurus (brack-e-uh-saw-rus)

Brontosaurus (bron-to-saw-rus)

Catastrophism (ca-tas-tro-fiz-um)

Clidastes tortor (cli-das-tees tor-tor)

Corythosaurus (cor-ith-uh-saw-rus)

Cretaceous (cre-tay-shus)

Cretoxyrhina (kre-tox-ae-rye-nah)

Cuvier (cue-vee-ay)

Dolichorhynchops (dol-i-co-rin-cups)

Dromaeosaurus (dro-me-uh-saw-rus)

Ectothermy (ec-to-therm-y)

Edmontosaurus (ed-mon-tuh-saw-rus)

Enchodus (en-ko-dus)

Endothermy (en-do-therm-y)

Eohippus (ee-oh-hip-us)

Gillicus (gil-lee-cuss)

Gondwana (gond-wa-na)

Hadrosaur (had-ruh-soar)

Hesperornis (hes-per-or-nis)

Homeothermy (ho-me-o-therm-y)

Hyracotherium (hy-rac-uh-theer-e-um)

Ichthyodectes (ick-thee-o-deck-tees)

Ichthyornis (ick-thee-or-nis)

Jurassic (ju-ras-ic) (did you really need help with this one?)

Kansius (kan-see-us)

Laurasia (lau-ray-sia)

Megalonyx (meg-a-lon-iks)

Mississippian (mis-i-sip-e-an)

Niobrara (ney-uh-brer-uh)

Niobrarasaurus (ney-uh-brer-uh-saw-rus)

Niobrarateuthis (ney-uh-brer-uh-too-thus)

Nodosaurs (no-doe-sawrs)

Nyctosaurus bonneri (nick-to-saw-rus bon-ner-i)

Pangea (pan-jee-a)

Panthalassa (pan-tha-las-sa)

Pennsylvanian (penn-syl-va-ne-an)

Permian (per-mee-an)

Plesiosaurs (pleas-ee-uh-saw-rus)

Poikilothermic (poi-ki-uh-therm-ic)

Protosphyraena (pro-toe-sfi-ree-nah)

Pteranodon sternbergi (ter-an-uh-don stern-berg-eye)

Pterodactyl (tear-uh-dack-tul)

Ptychodus (tie-coe-dus)

Quetzalcoatlus (quat-zal-co-at-lus)

Saurodon (sawr-uh-don)

Seismosaurus (size-mo-saw-rus)

Squalicorax (squa-luh-core-ax)

Stegoceras (steg-gos-uh-rus)

Supersaurus (su-per-saw-rus)

Triassic (tri-as-ic)

Triceratops (tri-ser-uh-tops)

Tylosaurus (tie-luh-saw-rus)

Tyrannosaurus rex (tie-ran-uh-saw-rus rex)

Uintacrinus (yew-in-tuh-cry-nus)

Ultrasaurus (Ul-tra-saw-rus)

Uniformitarianism (you-ne-for-mi-tear-i-uh-nizem)

Utahraptor (u-tah-rap-tor)

Velociraptor (ve-los-i-rap-tor)

Xiphactinus (zi-fact-in-us)

Partial List of References Consulted

Bardack, D. 1965. Anatomy and evolution of chirocentrid fishes. University of Kansas Paleontological Contributions Vertebrata 10:1–88.

Bartholomew, D. M. 1998. Pioneer Naturalist on the Plains: The Diary of Elam Bartholomew 1871–1934. Sunflower University Press, Manhattan, Kansas, 338 p.

Boardman, R. S., A. H. Cheetham, and A. J. Rowell (eds.). 1987. Fossil Invertebrates. Blackwell Scientific Publications, Palo Alto, California, 713 p.

Callaway, J. M and E. L. Nicholls (eds.). 1997. Ancient Marine Reptiles. Academic Press, San Diego, 501 p.

Carroll, R. L. 1988. Vertebrate Paleontology and Evolution. W. H. Freeman and Company, New York, 698 p.

Chin, K. and B. D. Gill. 1996. Dinosaurs, dung beetles, and conifers: Participants in a Cretaceous food web. Palaios 11:280–285.

Choate, J. R. 1977. Systematics collections at Fort Hays State University. Association for Systematics Collections Newsletter 5(6):61–64.

Choate, J. R. 1980. The Fort Hays State Museums. University Forum Fort Hays State University, Hays, Kansas, 22:5–9.

Collinson, M. E. 1990. Angiosperms. p. 79-84 *in* Palaeobiology: A Synthesis, D. E. G. Briggs and P. R. Crowther (eds.), Blackwell Scientific Publications, Cambridge, 583 p.

Dixon, D., B. Cox, R. J. G. Savage, and B. Gardiner. 1988. The MacMillan Illustrated Encyclopedia of Dinosaurs and Prehistoric Animals: A visual Who's Who of Prehistoric Life. MacMillan Publishing Company, New York, 312 p.

Felber, E. P., P. J. Currie, and J. Sovak. 1998. A Moment in Time with *Albertosaurus*. Troodon Productions, Inc., Alberta, Canada, 47 p.

Fenton, C. L. and M. A. Fenton, 1989. The Fossil Book: A Record of Prehistoric Life. Doubleday, New York, 740 p.

Forsythe, J. L. 1977. The First Seventy-Five Years: A History of Fort Hays State University 1902–1977. Fort Hays State University, Hays, Kansas, 296 p.

Frazier, W. J. and D. R. Schwimmer. 1987. Regional Stratigraphy of North America. Plenum Press, New York, 719 p.

Goody, P C. 1968. The skull of *Enchodus faujasi* from the Maastricht of southern Holland. II. Koninklijke Nederlandse Akademie van Wetenschappen 71(3):222–231.

Jaffe, M. 2000. The Gilded Dinosaur: The Fossil War Between E. D. Cope and O. C. Marsh and the Rise of American Science. Crown Publishers, New York, 424 p.

Kauffman, E. G. and N. F. Sohl. 1979. Rudists. p. 723–737 *in* Encyclopedia of Paleontology, R. W. Fairbridge and D. Jablonski (eds.), Dowden, Hutchinson, and Ross Inc., Stroudsburg, Pennsylvania, 886 p.

Kirkland, J. I., R. Gaston, and D. Burge. 1993. A large dromaeosaur (Theropoda) from the Lower Cretaceous of eastern Utah. Hunteria 2(10):1–16.

Lanham, U. 1973. The Bone Hunters: The Heroic Age of Paleontology in the American West. Dover Publications, New York, 285 p.

Madsen, J. H. Jr. 1976. *Allosaurus fragilis*: A revised osteology. Utah Geological and Mineral Survey Bulletin, 109:1–163.

McCarren, M. J. 1993. The Scientific Contributions of Othniel Charles Marsh: Birds, Bones, and Brontotheres. Peabody Museum of Natural History, New Haven, Connecticut, 66 p.

Merriam, D. F. 1963. The geologic history of Kansas. Kansas Geological Survey Bulletin 162:1–317.

Muir, L. E. 1981. Elam Bartholomew, Pioneer, Farmer, Botanist. Leonard Erle Muir, Stockton, Kansas. 85 p.

Norman, D. 1985. The Illustrated Encyclopedia of Dinosaurs. Crescent Books, New York, 208 p.

Rogers, K. 1991. The Sternberg Fossil Hunters: A Dinosaur Dynasty. Mountain Press Publishing, Missoula, Montana, 288 p.

Russell, D. A. 1967. Systematics and morphology of American mosasaurs. Peabody Museum of Natural History Bulletin, 23:1–250.

Savage, R. J. G. and M. R. Long. 1986. Mammal Evolution: An Illustrated Guide. Facts on File Publications, New York, 259 p.

Shimada, K. 1994. Paleobiology of the Late Cretaceous shark, *Cretoxyrhina mantelli* (Lamniformes: Cretoxyrhinidae), from Kansas. M. S. Thesis, Fort Hays State University, Hays, Kansas, 169 p.

Shimada, K. 1997. Paleoecological relationships of the Late Cretaceous lamniform shark, *Cretoxyrhina mantelli* (Agassiz). Journal of Paleontology 71(5):926-933.

Simpson, G. G. 1942. The beginnings of vertebrate paleontology in North America. Proceedings of the American Philosophical Society 86(1):130–188.

Sternberg, C. H. 1909. The Life of a Fossil Hunter. reprinted 1990, Indiana University Press, 286 p.

Sternberg, C. H. 1932. Hunting Dinosaurs in the Bad Lands of the Red Deer River Alberta, Canada, Published by the Author, San Diego, 261 p.

Sternberg, C. M. 1945. Pachycephalosauridae proposed for dome-headed dinosaurs, *Stegoceras lambei*, n. sp., described. Journal of Paleontology 19(5):534–538.

Sternberg, G. F. 1930. Thrills in fossil hunting. The Aerend 1(3):139–153.

Stewart, J. D. 1990. Niobrara Formation symbiotic fish in inoceramid bivalves. p 31–41 *in* Bennett, S. C. (ed.) Niobrara Chalk Excursion Guidebook, Museum of Natural History and the Kansas Geological Survey, Lawrence, Kansas 81 p.

Strickberger, M. W. 1990. Evolution. Jones and Bartlett Publishers, Boston, 579 p.

Thomasson, J. R. and M. R. Voorhies. 1990. Grasslands and grazers. p 84–87 *in* Palaeobiology: A Synthesis, D. E. G. Briggs and P. R. Crowther (eds.), Blackwell Scientific Publications, London, 583 p.

Turner, G. 1799. Memoir on the extraneous fossils, denominated mammoth bones: principally designed to shew, that they are the remains of more than one species of non-descript animal. Transactions of the American Philosophical Society, 4:510–518.

Wallace, D. R. 1999. The Bonehunters' Revenge: Dinosaurs, Greed, and the Greatest Scientific Feud of the Gilded Age. Houghton Mifflin Company, New York, 366 p.

Weier, T. E., C. R. Stocking, M. G. Barbour, and T. L. Rost. 1982. Botany: An Introduction to Plant Biology. Sixth Edition. John Wiley and Sons, New York, 720 p.

Weishampel, D. B., P. Dodson, and H. Osmolska (eds.). 1990. The Dinosauria. University of California Press, Berkeley, 733 p.

Wellnhofer, P. 1991. The Illustrated Encyclopedia of Pterosaurs. Salamander Books Ltd., London, 192 p.

Whittle, C. H. and M. J. Everhart. 2000. Apparent and implied evolutionary trends in lithophagic vertebrates from New Mexico and elsewhere. New Mexico Museum of Natural History and Science Bulletin, 17:75–82.

Wicander, R. and J. S. Monroe. 1989. Historical Geology: Evolution of the Earth and Life Through Time. West Publishing Company, New York, 578 p.

Witt, G. P. 1999. Clifton A. Witt. Grace P. Witt, Hays, Kansas.

Wooster, L. D. 1961. A History of Fort Hays Kansas State College 1902–1961. Fort Hays Kansas State College, Hays, Kansas, 200 p.

Index

Figure Credits

Cover: Photograph of the Sternberg Museum's *Tyrannosaurus* model by Charlie Riedel

Floor Plans of Museum. Modified from architutural drawing, photos by Greg and Cami Liggett

Kansas Geologic Map: used with permission from the Kansas Geological Survey

Figure 1. Photo by Mitch Weber

Figure 2–3. Forsyth Library, Fort Hays State University Archives, Hays, Kansas

Figures 4–5. By Greg Liggett

Figures 6–8. By Hannan LaGarry

Figure 9. By Greg Liggett

Figure 10. Forsyth Library, Fort Hays State University Archives, Hays, Kansas

Figure 11. Photo by Greg Liggett

Figures 12–15. Forsyth Library, Fort Hays State University Archives, Hays, Kansas

Figure 16–18. Courtesy of the Peabody Museum of Natural History, Yale University

Figure 19. Courtesy of the Peabody Museum of Natural History, Yale University

Figure 20. Photo by Greg Liggett

Figure 21. Courtesy of the Peabody Museum of Natural History, Yale University

Figure 22–24. Forsyth Library, Fort Hays State University Archives, Hays, Kansas

Figure 25. Negative number 35607, Courtesy of Department of Library Services, American Museum of Natural History

Figures 26. Forsyth Library, Fort Hays State University Archives, Hays, Kansas

Figures 27–29. Photo by Greg Liggett

Figures 30–31. Forsyth Library, Fort Hays State University Archives, Hays, Kansas

Figures 32–33. Photo by Greg Liggett

Figures 34–35. *Tyrannosaurus* illustrations based on Osborn, 1903. Crania of *Tyrannosaurus* and *Allosaurus*. American Museum of Natural History Memoirs, 1:1–30. *Allosaurus* illustrations based on Madsen, James H. Jr., 1976. *Allosaurus fragilis*: A revised osteology. Utah Geological and Mineral Survey Bulletin 109:1–163.

Figure 36. Forsyth Library, Fort Hays State University Archives, Hays, Kansas

Figure 37. By Greg Liggett

Figure 38. Cartoon by James Whitcraft printed in "Body mass, bone 'strength indicator,' and cursorial potential of *Tyrannosaurus rex*" by James O. Farlow, Matt B. Smith, and John M. Robinson in Journal of Vertebrate Paleontology vol. 15(4):713-725. Used with permission

Figure 39. Forsyth Library, Fort Hays State University Archives, Hays, Kansas

Figure 40. From Ratcliffe, 1999. New species of Canthonella Chapin (Scarabaeidae: Scarabaeinae) from Amazonian Brazil. The Coleopterists Bulletin 53(1):1–7. Used with permission of B. Ratcliffe and A. Smith, University of Nebraska State Museum

Figures 41–42. Photo by Greg Liggett

Figure 43. Modified from Collinson, 1990.

Figures 44–45. Photo by Greg Liggett

Figure 46. Redrawn by Greg Liggett from Thompson, Ernest E. 1896. Anatomy of Animals

Figure 47. Forsyth Library, Fort Hays State University Archives, Hays, Kansas

Figure 48. From the Sternberg Museum archives

Figure 49. Forsyth Library, Fort Hays State University Archives, Hays, Kansas

Figures 50–54. Photo by Greg Liggett

Figures 55–56. Forsyth Library, Fort Hays State University Archives, Hays, Kansas

Figure 57. Photo by Mitch Weber

Figure 58. Forsyth Library, Fort Hays State University Archives, Hays, Kansas

Figure 59. Drawn by Hannan LaGarry

Figure 60. Photo by Greg Liggett

Figure 61. Forsyth Library, Fort Hays State University Archives, Hays, Kansas

Figure 62. Drawn by Hannan LaGarry

Figure 63. Drawn by Kenshu Shimada

Figures 64–65. Photo by Greg Liggett

Figures 66–69. Forsyth Library, Fort Hays State University Archives, Hays, Kansas

Figure 70. Photo by Greg Liggett

Figure 71. Sternberg Museum archives

Figure 72. Photo by Greg Liggett

Figure 73. Forsyth Library, Fort Hays State University Archives, Hays, Kansas

Figure 74. From Russell, 1967

Figure 75. Forsyth Library, Fort Hays State University Archives, Hays, Kansas

Figure 76. From Russell, 1967

Figure 77. Drawn by Hannan LaGarry

Figure 78–79. Sternberg Museum archives

Figures 80–85. Photos by Greg Liggett

Figure 86. Forsyth Library, Fort Hays State University Archives, Hays, Kansas

Color Plate 1. Photo by Greg Liggett

Color Plate 2. Photo by Greg Liggett

Color Plate 3. Photo by Mitch Weber

Color Plate 4. Photo by Mitch Weber

Color Plate 5. Photo by Cami Liggett

Color Plate 6. Painting by Dan Varner

Color Plate 7. Painting by Dan Varner

Color Plate 8. Forsyth Library, Fort Hays State University Archives, Hays, Kansas, colored by Greg Liggett

Figure 87. Forsyth Library, Fort Hays State University Archives, Hays, Kansas

Figure 88. From the collection of the Sternberg Museum

Figures 89–91. Forsyth Library, Fort Hays State University Archives, Hays, Kansas

Figure 92–93. Photos by Mitch Weber

Figure 94–97. Forsyth Library, Fort Hays State University Archives, Hays, Kansas

Figure 98. Sternberg Museum archives

Figure 99–102. Forsyth Library, Fort Hays State University Archives, Hays, Kansas

Figure 103. Sternberg Museum archives

Figures 104–109. Photos by Greg Liggett

Figure 110. Photo by Greg Walters

The author examines the short-necked plesiosaur, Dolichorhynchops, *as it was mounted in the museum on the campus of Fort Hays State University before being moved to the dome.*

About the Author

Greg Liggett is presently the Assistant Director of the Sternberg Museum of Natural History in Hays, Kansas. He has a wide range of professional experience in diverse fields including medical technology, civil engineering, professional land surveying, biology and geology. Liggett has authored many publications of various kinds including scientific papers and lectures, and magazine, newspaper, and newsletter articles. He is a licensed professional geologist and is active in the Society of Vertebrate Paleontology, is a member of the American Society of Mammalogists, the Kansas Museums Association, and the Society for the Preservation of Natural History Collections. Liggett's on-going research interest is the prehistoric life of Kansas and the Great Plains.